The Psalms in Worship

THE PSALMS IN WORSHIP

*Arrangements from the Psalter
for Performance and Liturgy*

by
Paul M. Miller and Jeff Wyatt

Authors of *The Word in Worship*
and *Acts of Worship*

KANSAS CITY, MO 64141

Copyright © 1995
By Paul M. Miller and Jeff Wyatt

All print rights licensed by Lillenas Publishing Company
All rights reserved

PLEASE REMEMBER, this material is protected by copyright. Permission to reproduce the Scripture arrangements for worship services is granted with the inclusion of the permission line that appears with each selection.
Some minor adaptations and interpolations have been made in the wording of certain NIV passages, simply to insure clear communication within the script format.

Cover art by Paul Franitza

Scripture is from *The Holy Bible, New International Version.* Copyright © 1973, 1978, 1984 by the International Bible Society. Used by permission of Zondervan Bible Publishers. All rights reserved.

Contents

Preface 11

Readings

Psalm 1 15
    A Reading for Worship Leader and Congregation

Psalm 1 16
    A Reading for Worship Leader and Congregation

Psalm 1 17
    A Reading for Worship Leader and Congregation

Psalm 1 18
    A Reading for Worship Leader and Congregation

Psalm 2 19
    A Reading for Worship Leader, Congregation, and Two Solo Readers

Psalm 3 20
    A Reading for Worship Leader, Congregation, and Solo Reader

Psalm 3 21
    A Reading for Worship Leader, Choir, and Two Solo Readers

Psalm 4:1-4, 8 22
    A Reading for Choir and Two Solo Readers

Psalm 6:1-6, 8-9 23
    A Reading for Choir and Two Solo Readers

Psalm 8 24
    A Reading for Worship Leader and Congregation

Psalm 8 25
    A Reading for Worship Leader, Congregation, and Two Solo Readers

Psalm 9:1-14 26
    A Reading for Worship Leader, Congregation, and Two Solo Readers

Psalm 13 27
    A Reading for One Male and One Female Solo Reader

Psalm 14:1-6 28
    A Reading for Worship Leader and Congregation

Psalm 15 29
    A Reading for Worship Leader and Congregation

Psalm 16 30
    A Reading for Two Solo Readers

Psalm 18:1-6, 46-50 31
    A Reading for Worship Leader and One Male and
    One Female Solo Reader

Psalm 19:7-11 32
    A Reading for Worship Leader and Congregation
Psalm 22:1-2, 11, 19-23, 25-27, 29-31 33
    A Reading for Worship Leader, Men, and Male Solo Reader
Psalm 23:1-4 35
    A Readers Theatre Interpretation for Two Male and
    Two Female Solo Readers
Psalm 23 38
    A Readers Theatre Interpretation for Two Male and
    Two Female Solo Readers
Psalm 24 41
    A Reading for Worship Leader and Congregation
Psalms 27:1, 4-5, 7-9, 11-14; 91:1-4, 14-16 42
    A Reading for Worship Leader and Congregation
Psalm 29 44
    A Reading for Worship Leader and Congregation
Psalm 34:1-8 45
    A Reading for Worship Leader, Congregation, and Solo Reader
Psalm 36:5-9 46
    A Reading for Worship Leader, Choir, and Congregation
Psalm 37:1-11 47
    A Reading for Worship Leader and Congregation
Psalm 38 48
    A Reading for Two Solo Readers
Psalm 39 50
    A Reading for Worship Leader, Congregation, and Two Solo Readers
Psalm 40:1-5, 7-16 51
    A Reading for Worship Leader, Congregation, and Two Solo Readers
Psalm 42 53
    A Reading for Worship Leader and Three Solo Readers
Psalm 46 54
    A Reading for Worship Leader and Congregation
Psalm 47 55
    A Reading for Worship Leader and Congregation
Psalm 49 56
    A Reading for Worship Leader and Two Solo Readers
Psalm 51:1-17 58
    A Reading for Worship Leader, Choir, and Two Solo Readers
Psalm 53 60
    A Reading for Worship Leader and Congregation
Psalm 56 61
    A Reading for Choir and Two Solo Readers

Psalm 57 63
    A Reading for Worship Leader and Congregation
Psalm 61 64
    A Reading for Worship Leader and Congregation
Psalm 62 65
    A Reading for Two Solo Readers
Psalm 63 66
    A Reading for Two Solo Readers
Psalm 65 67
    A Reading for Worship Leader and Congregation
Psalm 66:1-4 68
    A Reading for Worship Leader and Congregation
Psalm 66:5-6 69
    A Reading for Worship Leader, Congregation, and Solo Reader
Psalm 66:8-10, 12 69
    A Reading for Worship Leader, Congregation, and Solo Reader
Psalm 66:16-20 70
    A Reading for Worship Leader, Congregation, and Solo Reader
Psalm 67:1-7 71
    A Reading for Worship Leader and Congregation
Psalm 71:9-15, 17-24 72
    A Reading for Worship Leader and Two Solo Readers
Psalm 73 74
    A Reading for Choir and Two Solo Readers
Psalm 78:1-4 77
    A Reading for Worship Leader and Congregation
Psalm 82 78
    A Reading for Worship Leader and Congregation
Psalm 84:1-4, 10-12 79
    A Reading for Worship Leader and Congregation
Psalm 86 80
    A Reading for Choir and Two Solo Readers
Psalm 88 81
    A Reading for Two Solo Readers
Psalm 89:5-18 83
    A Reading for Choir and Two Solo Readers
Psalm 90:1-4, 7-8, 10, 12, 17 84
    A Reading for Worship Leader and Two Solo Readers
Psalm 93 86
    A Reading for Worship Leader, Choir, and Congregation
Psalm 95:1-7 87
    A Reading for Worship Leader and Congregation
Psalm 97:1-6 88
    A Reading for Worship Leader, Choir, and Congregation
Psalm 100 89
    A Reading for Worship Leader, Choir, and Congregation

Psalm 103:1-5, 20-22 90
    A Reading for Worship Leader and Congregation
Psalm 103:8-18 91
    A Reading for Worship Leader and Congregation
Psalm 107:1 92
    A Reading for Worship Leader and Congregation
Psalm 107:2-11, 13-15, 22, 42-43 93
    A Reading for Worship Leader, Choir, and Two Solo Readers
Psalm 110 95
    A Reading for Worship Leader and Congregation
Psalm 111 96
    A Reading for Worship Leader and Congregation
Psalm 112:1-9 97
    A Reading for Worship Leader and Congregation
Psalm 113:1-8 98
    A Reading for Worship Leader and Congregation
Psalm 115 99
    A Reading for Worship Leader and Congregation
Psalm 117 100
    A Reading for Worship Leader and Congregation
Psalm 118 101
    A Reading for Worship Leader, Choir, and Five Solo Readers
Psalm 119:9-16 103
    A Reading for Male Worship Leader, Choir Men, and Teen Boy
Psalm 119:33-40 104
    A Reading for Worship Leader and Congregation
Psalm 119:41-48 105
    A Reading for Female Worship Leader, Choir Women, and
    Female Solo Reader
Psalm 119:105-112 106
    A Reading for Worship Leader and Congregation
Psalm 119:145-152 107
    A Reading for Worship Leader and Congregation
Psalm 121 108
    A Reading for Worship Leader, Choir, and Congregation
Psalm 121 109
    A Reading for Two Solo Readers
Psalm 122 110
    A Reading for Worship Leader and Congregation
Psalm 124 111
    A Reading for Two Solo Readers
Psalm 127 112
    A Reading for Worship Leader and Congregation

Psalm 128 113
    A Reading for Worship Leader and Congregation
Psalm 130 114
    A Reading for Worship Leader and Two Solo Readers
Psalm 133 115
    A Reading for Worship Leader and Congregation
Psalm 134 115
    A Reading for Worship Leader and Congregation
Psalm 136:1-18, 21-26 116
    A Reading for Worship Leader and Congregation
Psalm 137:1-6 118
    A Reading for Worship Leader and Two Solo Readers
Psalm 137 119
    A Readers Theatre Interpretation for Two Male and
    Two Female Solo Readers
Psalm 139:1-3, 23-24 122
    A Reading for Worship Leader and Congregation
Psalm 139:7-10 122
    A Reading for Worship Leader and Congregation
Psalm 144 123
    A Reading for Worship Leader and Congregation
Psalms 149:1-2, 4, 6; 67:4-5 125
    A Reading for Worship Leader and Congregation
Psalm 150 126
    A Reading for Worship Leader, Choir, Congregation, and
    Optional Instruments

Service Responses
Praise (134:1-2; 148:13-14) 127
Thanksgiving (30:2, 11-12) 127
Call to Worship (29:2; 100:2) 128
Call to Worship (19:14) 128
Call to Worship (118:24) 128
Call to Worship (34:3) 129
A Response (96:4) 129
A Response (84:11) 129

Topical Index 131

Preface

This is the third book in our *Word* series. Hopefully, it will be welcomed by worship leaders who agree with the authors that selections from the Psalms belong in traditional and contemporary worship services. The Psalms' poetic expressions of praise, thanksgiving, anguish, and confession speak to worshipers of every age and background. The Psalms' capability to express the hearts' cries of modern men and women is just as great as when David recognized his needy heart and wrote:

> Search me, O God, and know my heart;
>   test me and know my anxious thoughts.
> See if there is any offensive way in me,
>   and lead me in the way everlasting.
>   Psalm 139:23-24

Dietrich Bonhoeffer recognizes Psalms as "the great school of prayer." In the book *Life Together,** he reminds the reader, "The New Testament laid emphasis upon 'speaking to yourselves in psalms' (Eph. 5:19) and 'teaching and admonishing one another in psalms.'"

Worship planners ought to take Bonhoeffer's observation to heart. They need to provide opportunity for today's worshipers to hear and speak treasures from the Book of Psalms. That's what this book offers the liturgist or worship leader—a collection of psalm selections arranged to encourage participation in the Word.

All hymnals contain many much-loved selections with lyrics based on the songbook of the Bible. One of the oldest hymn lyrics based on Psalms is from the *Scottish Psalter* of 1650.

> The Lord's my Shepherd;
>   I'll not want.
> He makes me down to lie
>   In pastures green;
> He leadeth me
>   The quiet waters by.
>
> My soul He doth restore again,
>   And me to walk doth make
> Within the paths of righteousness,
>   E'en for His own name's sake.
>
> Yea, though I walk in death's dark vale,
>   Yet will I fear no ill;
> For Thou art with me, and Thy rod
>   And staff me comfort still.

My table Thou has furnished
  In presence of my foes;
My head Thou dost with oil anoint,
  And my cup over-flows.

Goodness and mercy all my life
  Shall surely follow me,
And in God's house forever more
  My dwelling place shall be.

To this day, many liturgical and some evangelical churches include reading, singing, and/or chanting the Psalter as part of their regular worship liturgy. At one time, in the Church of Scotland and other Calvinistic traditions, paraphrased psalms set to simple melodies were considered the only lyrics appropriate for divine worship. Today, in the midst of a worship revolution, when communicants are encouraged to express their faith in contemporary idioms, the inclusion of psalm reading is appropriate. Not only does it provide the worshiper with divinely inspired words of faith, but it provides a direct connection with the Church through the past 2,000 years.

We challenge you to offer your congregation the glorious opportunity to speak the Word, whether from resources derived from this book, or our other two Lillenas volumes, *The Word in Worship* and *Acts of Worship*, or from scripture arrangements you compose yourself.

* * *

Using These Psalm Arrangements

There are three types of psalm selections in this collection:

1. Arrangements to be read by the service leader, congregation, choir, and other designated readers. The emphasis is upon worship participation.

2. Scripted psalms featuring solo readers, which are to be rehearsed and presented in a worship service in the same way as a choral anthem.

3. Readers theatre scripts that include major portions of psalms, enhanced with dramatic vignettes and music.

Participation Readings

All of the selections in this book may be reproduced in a service folder or insert as long as the credit line that accompanies each is included.

While the congregation will be "sight reading" these selections in the service, it will be helpful if the worship leader, choir, and others will prepare their involvement. It is important that cues be picked up quickly, and the choir helps set the reading pace for the congregation.

Scripted Readings for Special Readers

Some of these readings call for solo readers. The participants should be selected ahead of the service and given an opportunity to prepare. On occasion it may replace a participation scripture reading or be introduced as a choir anthem. If you wish to include the congregation in one of these performances, select one of the voices (the choir or a soloist) and designate "People" for those readings, and print the piece as a handout. Please remember, if you retype any of the readings in this collection, include the permission line at the end of the selection.

Readers Theatre Readings

There are a few scripts in this collection that should be approached as worship theatre pieces. These must be thoroughly rehearsed. They may be performed as a scripture sketch from which a sermon is launched. The authors would like to hear from you regarding this use of scripture presentation.

* * *

We hope you make use of the topical index at the back of this volume. It is not exhaustive, but it will help you start selecting psalms for the theme of your worship, or, better yet, to correspond to the lectionary.

It is our hope and prayer that the Book of Psalms will become the source of great inspiration and dramatic intensity that it has become to us.

Paul M. Miller and Jeff Wyatt

Life Together, by Dietrich Bonhoeffer (Translated by John W. Doberson). New York: Harper and Row, 1954.

Readings

Psalm 1

LEADER: Blessed is the man

WOMEN: Blessed is the woman

ALL: Blessed is the person who does not walk in the counsel of the wicked

MEN: Or stand in the way of sinners

ALL: Or sit in the seat of mockers.

LEADER: But his delight is in the law of the Lord,

ALL: And on God's law he meditates day and night.

LEADER: Such a one is like a tree planted by streams of water,

WOMEN: Which yields its fruit in season

MEN: And whose leaf does not wither.

WOMEN: Whatever she does prospers.

MEN: Whatever he does prospers.

ALL: Whatever we do prospers.

LEADER: Not so the wicked! They are like chaff

ALL: That the wind blows away.

LEADER: Therefore the wicked will not stand in the judgment,

ALL: Nor sinners in the assembly of the righteous.

WOMEN: O Lord, watch over our ways.

MEN: O Lord, watch over our ways.

LEADER: For the Lord watches over the way of the righteous,

ALL: But the way of the wicked will perish.

LEADER: Blessed is the person

ALL: Who delights in the Lord.

Script and/or Scripture arrangement from *The Psalms in Worship*, by Miller and Wyatt, © 1995. All rights reserved by Lillenas Publishing Company. Scripture quotes and paraphrases are from the *Holy Bible, New International Version*® (NIV®). Copyright © 1973, 1978, 1984 by International Bible Society. Used by permission of Zondervan Publishing House. All rights reserved.

Psalm 1

LEADER: Oh, be a blessed person!

ALL: We will not walk with the wicked,

MEN: Or stand with sinners,

WOMEN: Or sit with the mockers.

LEADER: Delight in the law of the Lord. Meditate on it by day and night.

ALL: Then we shall be like a tree

MEN: Planted by streams of water,

WOMEN: Which yields its fruit in season

MEN: And whose leaf does not wither.

ALL: Whatever we do prospers.

LEADER: This is not so with the wicked!

WOMEN: The wicked are like chaff that the wind blows away.

ALL: Therefore the wicked will not stand in the judgment,

MEN: Nor will sinners stand in the assembly of the righteous.

LEADER: The Lord watches over the way of the righteous,

ALL: But the way of the wicked will perish.

MEN: We will delight in the law of the Lord.

WOMEN: We will meditate on his law day and night.

ALL: Whatever we do will prosper.

Script and/or Scripture arrangement from *The Psalms in Worship*, by Miller and Wyatt, © 1995. All rights reserved by Lillenas Publishing Company. Scripture quotes and paraphrases are from the *Holy Bible, New International Version*® (NIV®). Copyright © 1973, 1978, 1984 by International Bible Society. Used by permission of Zondervan Publishing House. All rights reserved.

Psalm 1

LEADER: Blessed is the man

ALL: Who does not walk in the counsel of the wicked

WOMEN: Or stand in the way of sinners

MEN: Or sit in the seat of mockers.

LEADER: But his delight is in the law of the Lord,

ALL: And on his law he meditates day and night.

WOMEN: He is like a tree planted by streams of water,

ALL: Which yields its fruit in season

MEN: And whose leaf does not wither.

ALL: Whatever he does prospers.

LEADER: Not so the wicked!

ALL: They are like chaff that the wind blows away.

LEADER: Therefore the wicked will not stand in judgment,

ALL: Nor sinners in the assembly of the righteous.

LEADER: For the Lord watches over the way of the righteous,

ALL: But the way of the wicked will perish.

Script and/or Scripture arrangement from *The Psalms in Worship*, by Miller and Wyatt, © 1995. All rights reserved by Lillenas Publishing Company. Scripture quotes and paraphrases are from the *Holy Bible, New International Version*® (NIV®). Copyright © 1973, 1978, 1984 by International Bible Society. Used by permission of Zondervan Publishing House. All rights reserved.

Psalm 1

LEADER: The Lord watches over the way of the righteous,

PEOPLE: But the way of the wicked will perish.

LEADER: Bles-sed is the man who does not walk in the counsel of the wicked

PEOPLE: The way of the wicked will perish!

LEADER: Bles-sed is the man who does not stand in the way of sinners.

PEOPLE: His delight is in the law of the Lord.

LEADER: Bles-sed is the man who does not sit in the seat of mockers.

PEOPLE: On the law of the Lord he meditates day and night.

LEADER: The blessed man is like a tree planted by streams of water, which yields its fruit in season and whose leaf does not wither.

PEOPLE: Not so the wicked!

LEADER: Whatever the blessed man does prospers.

PEOPLE: The wicked are like chaff that the wind blows away.

LEADER: Therefore the wicked will not stand in the judgment, nor sinners in the assembly of the righteous.

PEOPLE: The way of the wicked will perish.

LEADER: For the Lord watches over the way of the righteous,

PEOPLE: But the way of the wicked will perish.

Script and/or Scripture arrangement from *The Psalms in Worship*, by Miller and Wyatt, © 1995. All rights reserved by Lillenas Publishing Company. Scripture quotes and paraphrases are from the *Holy Bible, New International Version*® (NIV®). Copyright © 1973, 1978, 1984 by International Bible Society. Used by permission of Zondervan Publishing House. All rights reserved.

Psalm 2

LEFT: Why do the nations conspire?

RIGHT: The kings of the earth take their stand.

LEFT: Why do the peoples plot in vain?

RIGHT: The rulers gather together against the Lord and against his Anointed One.

SOLO 1: "Let us break their chains," they say.

LEADER: The One enthroned in heaven laughs.

SOLO 2: The Lord scoffs at them.

SOLO 1: "Let us throw off their fetters," they say.

LEADER: The Lord rebukes them in his anger

SOLO 2: The Lord terrifies them in his wrath, saying, "I have installed my King on Zion, my holy hill."

SOLO 1: I will proclaim the decree of the Lord: He said to me, "You are my Son; today I have become your Father. Ask of me, and I will make the nations your inheritance, the ends of the earth your possession. You will rule them with an iron scepter; you will dash them to pieces like pottery."

LEADER: Therefore, you kings, be wise; be warned, you rulers of the earth.

PEOPLE: Serve the Lord with fear and rejoice with trembling.

LEADER: Kiss the Son, lest he be angry and you be destroyed in your way, for his wrath can flare up in a moment.

PEOPLE: Blessed are all who take refuge in him.

Script and/or Scripture arrangement from *The Psalms in Worship*, by Miller and Wyatt, © 1995. All rights reserved by Lillenas Publishing Company. Scripture quotes and paraphrases are from the *Holy Bible, New International Version*® (NIV®). Copyright © 1973, 1978, 1984 by International Bible Society. Used by permission of Zondervan Publishing House. All rights reserved.

Psalm 3

LEADER: This is a psalm of David when he needed confidence.

SOLO 1: O Lord, how many are my foes! How many rise up against me! Many are saying of me,

WOMEN: "God will not deliver him."

SOLO 1: But you are a shield around me, O Lord; you bestow glory on me and lift up my head.

MEN: To the Lord I cry aloud,

WOMEN: And he answers me from his holy hill.

LEADER: This is a psalm of David when he needed protection.

SOLO 1: I lie down and sleep; I wake up again, because the Lord sustains me.

MEN: I will not fear the tens of thousands drawn up against me on every side.

LEADER: This is a psalm of David when he needed to know God's justice.

SOLO 1: Arise, O Lord! Deliver me, O my God!

WOMEN: Strike all my enemies on the jaw;

MEN: Break the teeth of the wicked.

LEADER: From the Lord comes deliverance.

ALL: May your blessing be on your people.

Script and/or Scripture arrangement from *The Psalms in Worship*, by Miller and Wyatt, © 1995. All rights reserved by Lillenas Publishing Company. Scripture quotes and paraphrases are from the *Holy Bible, New International Version*® (NIV®). Copyright © 1973, 1978, 1984 by International Bible Society. Used by permission of Zondervan Publishing House. All rights reserved.

Psalm 3

LEADER: From the Lord comes deliverance.

CHOIR: May your blessing be on your people.

SOLO 1: O Lord, how many are my foes! How many rise up against me!

SOLO 2: You are a shield around me, O Lord.

SOLO 1: Many are saying of me, "God will not deliver him."

SOLO 2: You bestow glory on me and lift up my head.

SOLO 1: To the Lord I cry aloud,

SOLO 2: And he answers from his holy hill.

SOLO 1: I lie down and sleep;

SOLO 2: I wake again, because the Lord sustains me.

LEADER: From the Lord comes deliverance.

CHOIR: May your blessing be on your people.

Script and/or Scripture arrangement from *The Psalms in Worship,* by Miller and Wyatt, © 1995. All rights reserved by Lillenas Publishing Company. Scripture quotes and paraphrases are from the *Holy Bible, New International Version*® (NIV®). Copyright © 1973, 1978, 1984 by International Bible Society. Used by permission of Zondervan Publishing House. All rights reserved.

Psalm 4

(vv. 1-4, 8)

CHOIR MEN: O my righteous God . . .

CHOIR WOMEN: Answer me when I call to you.

CHOIR MEN: O my righteous God . . .

CHOIR WOMEN: Give me relief from my distress;

SOLO 1: Be merciful to me and hear my prayer.

CHOIR MEN: How long, O men . . .

CHOIR WOMEN: Will you turn my glory into shame?

CHOIR MEN: How long will you love delusions

CHOIR WOMEN: And seek false gods?

SOLO 2: Know that the Lord has set apart the godly for himself;

SOLO 1: The Lord will hear when I call to him.

SOLO 2: In your anger do not sin; when you are on your beds, search your hearts and be silent.

SOLO 1: I will lie down and sleep in peace, for you alone, O Lord, make me dwell in safety.

CHOIR MEN: O Lord . . .

CHOIR WOMEN: Let the light of your face . . .

SOLO 2: Let the light of your face shine upon us, O Lord.

Script and/or Scripture arrangement from *The Psalms in Worship*, by Miller and Wyatt, © 1995. All rights reserved by Lillenas Publishing Company. Scripture quotes and paraphrases are from the *Holy Bible, New International Version*® (NIV®). Copyright © 1973, 1978, 1984 by International Bible Society. Used by permission of Zondervan Publishing House. All rights reserved.

Psalm 6

(vv. 1-6, 8-9)

Solo 1: O Lord, do not rebuke me in your anger or discipline me in your wrath.

Solo 2: Be merciful to me, Lord, for I am faint.

Choir: How long, O Lord, how long?

Solo 1: O Lord, heal me, for my bones are in agony.

Solo 2: My soul is in anguish.

Choir: How long, O Lord, how long?

Solo 1: Turn, O Lord, and deliver me;

Solo 2: Save me because of your unfailing love.

Choir: How long, O Lord, how long?

Solo 1: No one remembers you when he is dead.

Solo 2: Who praises you from the grave?

Choir: How long, O Lord, how long?

Solo 1: I am worn out from groaning;

Solo 2: All night long I flood my bed with weeping and drench my couch with tears.

Choir: How long, O Lord, how long?

Solo 1: Away from me, all you who do evil,

Choir: Away!

Solo 2: The Lord has heard my weeping.

Choir: The Lord has heard . . .

Solo 1: The Lord has heard my cry for mercy;

Choir: The Lord has heard!

Solo 2: The Lord accepts my prayer.

Script and/or Scripture arrangement from *The Psalms in Worship,* by Miller and Wyatt, © 1995. All rights reserved by Lillenas Publishing Company. Scripture quotes and paraphrases are from the *Holy Bible, New International Version*® (NIV®). Copyright © 1973, 1978, 1984 by International Bible Society. Used by permission of Zondervan Publishing House. All rights reserved.

Psalm 8

LEADER: It is a praising psalmist who declares, O Lord, our Lord,

ALL: How majestic is your name in all the earth!

MEN: You have set your glory above the heavens.

WOMEN: From the lips of children and infants you have ordained praise.

LEADER: When I consider your heavens,

MEN: The work of your fingers,

WOMEN: The moon and the stars, which you have set into place,

MEN: What is man that you are mindful of him,

WOMEN: The son of man that you care for him?

LEADER: You made him a little lower than the heavenly beings

ALL: And crowned him with glory and honor.

LEADER: You made him ruler over the works of your hands; you put everything under his feet:

WOMEN: All the flocks and herds,

MEN: And the beasts of the field,

WOMEN: The birds of the air,

MEN: And the fish of the sea,

ALL: All that swim the paths of the seas.

LEADER: The praising psalmist continues: O Lord, our Lord,

ALL: How majestic is your name in all the earth!

Script and/or Scripture arrangement from *The Psalms in Worship,* by Miller and Wyatt, © 1995. All rights reserved by Lillenas Publishing Company. Scripture quotes and paraphrases are from the *Holy Bible, New International Version*® (NIV®). Copyright © 1973, 1978, 1984 by International Bible Society. Used by permission of Zondervan Publishing House. All rights reserved.

Psalm 8

LEADER: O Lord!

PEOPLE: Our Lord!

LEADER: O Lord, how majestic is your name in all the earth!

PEOPLE: You have set your glory above the heavens.

SOLO 1: Lord, when I consider . . .

SOLO 2: When I consider your heavens,

SOLO 1: The work of your fingers, O Lord,

SOLO 2: When I consider the moon and the stars, which you have set in place,

SOLO 1: O Lord, when I consider . . .

SOLO 2: What is man that you are mindful of him?

SOLO 1: O Lord, when I consider . . .

SOLO 2: What is the son of man that you care for him?

SOLO 1: You made him a little lower than the heavenly beings.

SOLO 2: You crowned him with glory and honor.

LEADER: O Lord,

PEOPLE: Our Lord, how majestic is your name!

SOLO 1: You made him ruler over the works of your hands.

SOLO 2: You put everything under his feet:

SOLO 1: All flocks and herds, and the beasts of the field,

SOLO 2: The birds of the air, and the fish of the sea, all that swim the paths of the seas.

LEADER: O Lord,

PEOPLE: Our Lord,

LEADER: How majestic is your name . . .

PEOPLE: . . . in all the earth!

Script and/or Scripture arrangement from *The Psalms in Worship,* by Miller and Wyatt, © 1995. All rights reserved by Lillenas Publishing Company. Scripture quotes and paraphrases are from the *Holy Bible, New International Version*® (NIV®). Copyright © 1973, 1978, 1984 by International Bible Society. Used by permission of Zondervan Publishing House. All rights reserved.

Psalm 9

(vv. 1-14)

LEADER: David composed the ninth psalm for the director of music. It is a kingly song of praise for God's deliverance and care. I will praise you, O Lord, with all my heart;

PEOPLE: I will praise you, O Lord, with all my heart;

LEADER: I will praise you, O Lord; I will tell of all your wonders.

PEOPLE: I will praise you, O Lord; I will be glad and rejoice in you;

LEADER: I will sing praise to your name,

PEOPLE: I will sing praise to your name, O Most High.

SOLO 1: My enemies turn back; they stumble and perish before you. For you have upheld my right and my cause; you have sat on your throne, judging righteously. You have rebuked the nations and destroyed the wicked; you have blotted out their name for ever and ever.

SOLO 2: Endless ruin has overtaken the enemy, you have uprooted their cities; even the memory of them has perished.

LEADER: The Lord reigns forever;

PEOPLE: The Lord has established his throne for judgment.

LEADER: The Lord will judge the world in righteousness;

PEOPLE: The Lord will govern the peoples with justice.

SOLO 1: The Lord is a refuge for the oppressed, a stronghold in times of trouble.

SOLO 2: Those who know your name will trust in you, for you, Lord, have never forsaken those who seek you.

LEADER: Sing praises to the Lord,

PEOPLE: Enthroned in Zion;

LEADER: Sing praises to the Lord;

PEOPLE: Proclaim among the nations what he has done.

LEADER: Sing praises to the Lord;

PEOPLE: He does not ignore the cry of the afflicted.

LEADER: O Lord, have mercy and lift me up from the gates of death, that I may declare your praises in the gates of the Daughter of Zion

PEOPLE: And there rejoice in your salvation.

Script and/or Scripture arrangement from *The Psalms in Worship*, by Miller and Wyatt, © 1995. All rights reserved by Lillenas Publishing Company. Scripture quotes and paraphrases are from the *Holy Bible, New International Version*® (NIV®). Copyright © 1973, 1978, 1984 by International Bible Society. Used by permission of Zondervan Publishing House. All rights reserved.

Psalm 13

SOLO WOMAN: How long, O Lord?

SOLO MAN: Will you forget me forever?

SOLO WOMAN: How long will you hide your face from me?

SOLO MAN: How long must I wrestle with my thoughts and every day have sorrow in my heart?

SOLO WOMAN: How long will my enemy triumph over me?

SOLO MAN: Look on me and answer, O Lord my God.

SOLO WOMAN: Give light to my eyes, or I will sleep in death;

SOLO MAN: My enemy will say, "I have overcome him," and my foes will rejoice when I fall.

SOLO WOMAN: But I trust in your unfailing love; my heart rejoices in your salvation.

SOLO MAN: I will sing to the Lord, for he has been good to me.

Script and/or Scripture arrangement from *The Psalms in Worship*, by Miller and Wyatt, © 1995. All rights reserved by Lillenas Publishing Company. Scripture quotes and paraphrases are from the *Holy Bible, New International Version*® (NIV®). Copyright © 1973, 1978, 1984 by International Bible Society. Used by permission of Zondervan Publishing House. All rights reserved.

Psalm 14

(vv. 1-6)

LEADER: The fool says in his heart, "There is no God."

PEOPLE: They are corrupt, their deeds are vile; there is no one who does good.

LEADER: The Lord looks down from heaven on the sons of men to see if there are any who understand, any who seek God.

PEOPLE: All have turned aside, they have together become corrupt; there is no one who does good, not even one.

LEADER: Will evildoers never learn—those who devour my people as men eat bread and who do not call on the Lord?

PEOPLE: There they are, overwhelmed with dread, for God is present in the company of the righteous.

LEADER: You evildoers frustrate the plans of the poor,

PEOPLE: But the Lord is their refuge.

Script and/or Scripture arrangement from *The Psalms in Worship*, by Miller and Wyatt, © 1995. All rights reserved by Lillenas Publishing Company. Scripture quotes and paraphrases are from the *Holy Bible, New International Version*® (NIV®). Copyright © 1973, 1978, 1984 by International Bible Society. Used by permission of Zondervan Publishing House. All rights reserved.

Psalm 15

LEADER: Lord, who may dwell in your sanctuary?

ALL: Who may live on your holy hill?

RIGHT: He whose walk is blameless

LEFT: And who does what is righteous,

RIGHT: Who speaks the truth from his heart,

LEFT: Who has no slander on his tongue,

RIGHT: Who does his neighbor no wrong and casts no slur on his fellowman,

LEFT: Who despises a vile man but honors those who fear the Lord,

RIGHT: Who keeps his oath even when it hurts,

LEFT: Who lends his money without usury and does not accept a bribe against the innocent.

ALL: He who does these things will never be shaken.

Script and/or Scripture arrangement from *The Psalms in Worship*, by Miller and Wyatt, © 1995. All rights reserved by Lillenas Publishing Company. Scripture quotes and paraphrases are from the *Holy Bible, New International Version*® (NIV®). Copyright © 1973, 1978, 1984 by International Bible Society. Used by permission of Zondervan Publishing House. All rights reserved.

Psalm 16

Solo 1: Keep me safe, O God, for in you I take refuge.

Solo 2: I said to the Lord, "You are my Lord; apart from you I have no good thing."

Solo 1: As for the saints who are in the land, they are the glorious ones in whom is all my delight.

Solo 2: The sorrows of those will increase who run after other gods.

Solo 1: Lord, you have assigned me my portion and my cup;

Solo 2: You have made my lot secure.

Solo 1: The boundary lines have fallen for me in pleasant places;

Solo 2: Surely I have a delightful inheritance.

Solo 1: I will praise the Lord, who counsels me;

Solo 2: Even at night my heart instructs me.

Solo 1: I have set the Lord always before me.

Solo 2: Because he is at my right hand, I will not be shaken.

Solo 1: Therefore my heart is glad and my tongue rejoices;

Solo 2: My body also will rest secure,

Solo 1: Because you will not abandon me to the grave,

Solo 2: Nor will you let your Holy One see decay.

Solo 1: You have made known to me the path of life;

Solo 2: You will fill me with joy in your presence, with eternal pleasures at your right hand.

Script and/or Scripture arrangement from *The Psalms in Worship,* by Miller and Wyatt, © 1995. All rights reserved by Lillenas Publishing Company. Scripture quotes and paraphrases are from the *Holy Bible, New International Version*® (NIV®). Copyright © 1973, 1978, 1984 by International Bible Society. Used by permission of Zondervan Publishing House. All rights reserved.

Psalm 18

(vv. 1-6, 46-50)

Solo Woman: I love you, O Lord, my strength.

Solo Man: The Lord is my rock, my fortress and my deliverer;

Solo Man and Woman: My God is my rock, in whom I take refuge.

Solo Man: He is my shield and the horn of my salvation,

Solo Woman: My stronghold.

Leader: I call to the Lord, who is worthy of praise,

All: And I am saved from my enemies.

Solo Man: The cords of death entangled me;

Solo Woman: The torrents of destruction overwhelmed me.

Solo Man: The cords of the grave coiled around me;

Solo Woman and Man: The snares of death confronted me.

Solo Woman: In my distress I called to the Lord;

Solo Man: I cried to my God for help.

Leader: From his temple he heard my voice;

All: My cry came before him, into my ears.

Solo Man: The Lord lives!

Solo Woman: Praise be to my Rock!

Solo Man: He is the God who saves me from my enemies.

Solo Woman: You exalted me above my foes;

Solo Man and Woman: From violent men you rescued me.

Leader: Therefore I will praise you among the nations, O Lord;

All: I will sing praises to your name.

Leader: He shows unfailing kindness to his anointed,

All: And his descendants forever.

Script and/or Scripture arrangement from *The Psalms in Worship*, by Miller and Wyatt, © 1995. All rights reserved by Lillenas Publishing Company. Scripture quotes and paraphrases are from the *Holy Bible, New International Version*® (NIV®). Copyright © 1973, 1978, 1984 by International Bible Society. Used by permission of Zondervan Publishing House. All rights reserved.

Psalm 19

(vv. 7-11)

LEADER: The law of the Lord is perfect,

PEOPLE: Reviving the soul.

LEADER: The statutes of the Lord are trustworthy,

PEOPLE: Making wise the simple.

LEADER: The precepts of the Lord are right,

PEOPLE: Giving joy to the heart.

LEADER: The commands of the Lord are radiant,

PEOPLE: Giving light to the eyes.

LEADER: The fear of the Lord is pure,

PEOPLE: Enduring forever.

LEADER: The ordinances of the Lord are sure

PEOPLE: And altogether righteous.

LEADER: They are more precious than gold,

PEOPLE: Than much pure gold;

LEADER: They are sweeter than honey,

PEOPLE: Than honey from the comb.

LEADER: By them is your servant warned;

PEOPLE: In keeping them there is great reward.

Script and/or Scripture arrangement from *The Psalms in Worship,* by Miller and Wyatt, © 1995. All rights reserved by Lillenas Publishing Company. Scripture quotes and paraphrases are from the *Holy Bible, New International Version®* (NIV®). Copyright © 1973, 1978, 1984 by International Bible Society. Used by permission of Zondervan Publishing House. All rights reserved.

Psalm 22

(vv. 1-2, 11, 19-23, 25-27, 29-31)

LEADER: Hear these words ascribed to David.

SOLO MAN: My God,

MEN: My God,

SOLO MAN: Why?

MEN: Why have you forsaken me?

SOLO MAN: Why are you so far from saving me,

MEN: So far from the words of my groaning?

SOLO MAN: O my God,

MEN: O my God, I cry out by day,

SOLO MAN: But you do not answer,

MEN: By night, and am not silent.

SOLO MAN: Do not be far from me,

MEN: For trouble is near and there is no one to help.

SOLO MAN: O Lord, be not far off;

MEN: O my Strength, come quickly to help me.

LEADER: Deliver my life from the sword.

MEN: Rescue me from the mouths of the lions.

SOLO MAN: I will declare your name to my brothers;

MEN: In the congregation I will praise you.

SOLO MAN: You who fear the Lord, praise him!

MEN: All you descendants of Jacob, honor him!

SOLO MAN: Revere him, all you descendants of Israel!

LEADER: From you comes the theme of my praise in the great assembly.

SOLO MAN: The poor will eat and be satisfied;

MEN: They who seek the Lord will praise him.

SOLO MAN: All the ends of the earth will remember and turn to the Lord,

MEN: All the families of the nations will bow down before him.

SOLO MAN: All the rich of the earth will feast and worship;

MEN: All who go down to the dust will kneel before him.

SOLO MAN: Posterity will serve him;

MEN: Future generations will be told about the Lord.

SOLO MAN: They will proclaim his righteousness to a people yet unborn—

ALL: For he has done it.

Script and/or Scripture arrangement from *The Psalms in Worship,* by Miller and Wyatt, © 1995. All rights reserved by Lillenas Publishing Company. Scripture quotes and paraphrases are from the *Holy Bible, New International Version*® (NIV®). Copyright © 1973, 1978, 1984 by International Bible Society. Used by permission of Zondervan Publishing House. All rights reserved.

Green Pastures
Psalm 23:1-4

A Readers Theatre Interpretation

MAN 1 *(writing):* So, journal, as you already know, this starts my third week as apprentice sheep wrangler and almost-got-the-hang-of-it fence mender. Actually, the sheep and I are near strangers, except for the times I've had to chase down some strays who'd wandered off through openings where fence wire was down.

    Last night I decided the bunk trailer was too stuffy, so I brought my sleeping bag out here next to the coals of our campfire. It is already pretty cold for these end-days of summer. The minute the sun goes down behind the Sangre de Cristos, this high plain pasture takes on a chill that makes the old army blanket inside my bag feel pretty good.

    Because the sheep pen is just a stone's throw from me, I am very conscious of every sound the animals make, and of the night sounds. I strain to hear sounds of predators that can be lurking around the edges of a sheep outpost like this. Another rancher in the vicinity has had to fight off a pack of coyotes for the past several nights. I don't know what I'd do if I had to scare off coyotes. Let's hope I never have to find out.

[Soloist or congregation may sing the first stanza of "Savior, like a Shepherd Lead Us."]

WOMAN 1: The Lord is my shepherd, I shall not be in want. He makes me lie down in green pastures, he leads me beside quiet waters.

MAN 2: Now a certain Jesse of Bethlehem had eight sons. There was Eliab, Abinadab, Shammah, four others, and the child of the family, David.

WOMAN 2: David was the youngest of Jesse's eight boys. While his brothers did men's work, David cared for his father's flock of sheep.

MAN 2: "But when can I have a man's job, Father? Like my brothers?" David often asked old Jesse.

WOMAN 2: His father's answer was always the same, "You are doing necessary work, my son. Be faithful in small things."

Man 2: "But, Father, I want to prove myself a man. Give me something important to do. Let me show you how brave I am."

Woman 2: And brave he was. As a shepherd, the youngest of Jesse's boys learned to use what was in his hand, a sling and stones, to protect his father's sheep from predators, and Israel from a giant Philistine.

Woman 1: He leads me beside quiet waters, he restores my soul.

Woman 2: He guides me in paths of righteousness for his name's sake.

Man 2: Even though I walk through the valley of the shadow of death,

Man 1 *(writing in journal):* "I will fear no evil." The fire coals are almost gone, and there's a stirring in the trees—night winds make the animals restless. But as for me, all wrapped in my sleeping bag and lying here in this green pasture, I listen to the sheep sounds coming from the pen behind me; I think about tomorrow and how I will have to move them to another grazing spot. We'll have to cross the highway, but my sheep need not fear. I'll take good care of them.

[Soloist or congregation may sing the second stanza of "Savior, like a Shepherd Lead Us."]

Woman 2: Early one morning, Jesse came to David and explained that Eliab had taken a count of the sheep already that morning, and reported they were short at least one animal. "When they're herded into the fold tonight," Jesse requested, "you count them, David. I think you're better acquainted with your sheep." So that night, David stood by the door of the sheep fold . . .

Man 2: 97, 98, 99 . . .

Woman 2: David's eyes darted through the flock.

Man 2: There *is* a sheep missing. The lamb with the black patch on her face isn't with her mother.

Woman 2: With that, David grabbed the hooked staff that leaned against the sheep pen and took off through the gathering night to find the lost lamb with a black patch on her face.

Man 2: Little lamb, where you are, do not fear the night. Even in the shadows of night, I will find you. Fear no evil. With my hooked staff I will find you and will comfort you, little lamb.

Woman 1: I will fear no evil, for you are with me; your rod and your staff, they comfort me.

MAN 1 *(writing):* The beat of a shepherd's heart is heard in these words of poet Robert Blake.

> *And now beside thee, bleating lamb,*
>   *I can lie down and sleep,*
> *Or think on Him who bore thy name,*
>   *Graze after thee, and weep.*
> *For, wash'd in life's river,*
> *My bright mane for ever*
> *Shall shine like the gold*
> *As I guard o'er the fold.*

[Soloist or congregation may sing the third stanza of "Savior, like a Shepherd Lead Us."]

Script and/or Scripture arrangement from *The Psalms in Worship*, by Miller and Wyatt, © 1995. All rights reserved by Lillenas Publishing Company. Scripture quotes and paraphrases are from the *Holy Bible, New International Version*® (NIV®). Copyright © 1973, 1978, 1984 by International Bible Society. Used by permission of Zondervan Publishing House. All rights reserved.

In the House of the Lord
Psalm 23

A Readers Theatre Interpretation

WOMAN 1: The Lord is my shepherd,

MAN 2: I shall not be in want.

WOMAN 1: He makes me lie down in green pastures,

WOMAN 2: He leads me beside quiet waters,

MAN 1: He restores my soul.

WOMAN 1: He guides me in paths of righteousness

MAN 2: For his name's sake.

WOMAN 1: Even though I walk through the valley of the shadow of death,

WOMAN 2: I will fear no evil,

MAN 2: For you are with me;

WOMAN 1: Your rod and your staff,

ALL: They comfort me.

MAN 1 *(writing):* Here I am again, dear journal; still the sheep-meister that I was last time I wrote. Fence mending has been finished for a few weeks, so I have been devoting all my time to nearly 100 of the most unintelligent creatures on the face of God's green earth.

    The other evening I had to lift a lamb from a precarious rock outcropping. While I was trying to reach him with my staff, I had to smile; the tableaux was like a Sunday School Christmas pageant—except I was wearing jeans and a flannel shirt, not Dad's bathrobe. When I finally was able to pull the little guy up and onto sure footing, he was so shaky that I picked him up and carried him back to the pen.

    These sheep are always hungry. When they're not foraging the grass and bushes, they're chomping down mash from their feeding trough—kind of a manger, if you please. My appetite is ravenous too. Every noon, if I'm close enough to the main house, we eat a huge dinner. All the hired help sit around a spread that could feed three times the number eating. I like the idea that the needs of both the sheep and us humans are being met.

[Soloist or congregation may sing the first stanza "O Thou in Whose Presence."]

Woman 1: You prepare a table before me in the presence of my enemies.

Man 2: You anoint my head with oil;

Woman 2: My cup overflows.

Man 2: Thank You, God, for my bountiful table . . .

Woman 2: Thank You, God, for the oil of Your blessing.

Woman 1: I am reminded of Your provisions,

Man 1: Your care . . .

Woman 2: Your concern . . .

Man 2: Your everlasting concern for my welfare.

All: My cup overflows!

Woman 1: My cup of good things.

Man 1: My cup of thanksgiving.

Woman 2: My cup of forgiveness.

Man 2: My cup of joy.

All: Surely goodness and love will follow me all the days of my life.

[Soloist or congregation may sing the second stanza of "O Thou in Whose Presence."]

Man 1: Another night is coming on. I can see lights through the windows of a farmhouse north of me. I can't help but think of the family in there gathering around the kitchen table. The dad is probably still washing up from the chores of the day, and his wife is scolding him for being late, "'cuz the dinner's getting cold."

    In my first week on this job, I got lost coming back from the pasture farthest out. It was getting dark and cold. I'm not sure where I took a wrong turn, but I really had no idea where I was. I was lost. But when I saw a gleam of yellow light and smoke drifting up and out of a familiar chimney, I knew exactly where I was. I could just imagine that kitchen with a circle of happy family members circling the table, and thought I could smell the aroma of pot roast, green beans, mashed potatoes, and Aunt Molly's specialty, hot Dutch apple pie à la mode.

    Funny, when I saw that kitchen window with its light spilling out into the yard with a beckoning warm glow, I lost all my apprehension and fear of what Uncle Bill and his boys would say. I just wanted to get home.

Woman 2: Surely goodness and love will follow me . . .

Man 2: Will follow me all the days of my life,

Woman 1: Surely goodness and love will follow me all the days of my life.

All: And I will dwell in the house of the Lord forever.

[Soloist or congregation may sing the fifth stanza of "O Thou in Whose Presence."]

Script and/or Scripture arrangement from *The Psalms in Worship,* by Miller and Wyatt, © 1995. All rights reserved by Lillenas Publishing Company. Scripture quotes and paraphrases are from the *Holy Bible, New International Version*® (NIV®). Copyright © 1973, 1978, 1984 by International Bible Society. Used by permission of Zondervan Publishing House. All rights reserved.

Psalm 24

LEADER: The earth is the Lord's,

ALL: And everything in it,

LEADER: The world,

ALL: And all who live in it;

MEN: For he founded it upon the seas

ALL: And established it upon the waters.

LEADER: Who may ascend the hill of the Lord?

WOMEN: Who may stand in his holy place?

LEADER: He who has clean hands and a pure heart,

MEN: Who does not lift up his soul to an idol

WOMEN: Or swear by what is false.

LEADER: He will receive blessing from the Lord and vindication from God his Savior. Such is the generation of those who seek him,

ALL: Who seek your face, O God of Jacob.

LEADER: Lift up your heads, O you gates;

WOMEN: Be lifted up, you ancient doors,

MEN: That the King of glory may come in.

ALL: Who is this King of glory?

WOMEN: The Lord strong and mighty,

MEN: The Lord mighty in battle.

LEADER: Lift up your heads, O you gates; lift them up, you ancient doors,

ALL: That the King of glory may come in.

MEN: Who is he,

WOMEN: This King of glory?

LEADER: The Lord Almighty—

ALL: He is the King of glory.

Script and/or Scripture arrangement from *The Psalms in Worship*, by Miller and Wyatt, © 1995. All rights reserved by Lillenas Publishing Company. Scripture quotes and paraphrases are from the *Holy Bible, New International Version*® (NIV®). Copyright © 1973, 1978, 1984 by International Bible Society. Used by permission of Zondervan Publishing House. All rights reserved.

Psalms 27 and 91

(27:1, 4-5, 7-9, 11-14; 91:1-4, 14-16)

LEADER: The Lord is my light and my salvation—

ALL: Whom shall I fear?

MEN: The Lord is the stronghold of my life—

ALL: Of whom shall I be afraid?

LEADER: He who dwells in the shelter of the Most High will rest in the shadow of the Almighty.

WOMEN: One thing I ask of the Lord, this is what I seek:

ALL: That I may dwell in the house of the Lord all the days of my life.

MEN: I will say of the Lord, "He is my refuge and my fortress, my God, in whom I trust."

LEADER: In the day of trouble he will keep me safe in his dwelling;

WOMEN: He will hide me in the shelter of his tabernacle

ALL: And set me high upon a rock.

LEADER: He will save [me] from the fowler's snare and from deadly pestilence.

MEN: He will cover [me] with his feathers,

WOMEN: And under his wings [I] will find refuge;

ALL: His faithfulness will be [my] shield and rampart.

LEADER: Hear my voice when I call, O Lord;

MEN: Be merciful to me and answer me.

LEADER: My heart says of you, "Seek his face!"

WOMEN: Your face, Lord, I will seek.

MEN: Do not hide your face from me,

WOMEN: Do not reject me or forsake me,

MEN: Do not turn me over to the desire of my foes.

ALL: Teach me your way, O Lord; lead me in a straight path.

LEADER: The Lord says,

MEN: "Because [you] love me, I will rescue [you].

WOMEN: "I will protect [you], for [you] acknowledge my name.

MEN: "I will be with [you] in trouble,

WOMEN: "I will deliver [you] and honor [you]

LEADER: "You will call upon me, and I will answer."

MEN: I am still confident of this:

ALL: I will see the goodness of the Lord.

LEADER: "With long life I will satisfy [you]

ALL: "And show [you] my salvation."

LEADER: Wait for the Lord;

MEN: Be strong,

WOMEN: Take heart,

ALL: Wait for the Lord.

Script and/or Scripture arrangement from *The Psalms in Worship,* by Miller and Wyatt, © 1995. All rights reserved by Lillenas Publishing Company. Scripture quotes and paraphrases are from the *Holy Bible, New International Version*® (NIV®). Copyright © 1973, 1978, 1984 by International Bible Society. Used by permission of Zondervan Publishing House. All rights reserved.

Psalm 29

LEADER: Ascribe to the Lord,

PEOPLE: Ascribe to the Lord glory and strength.

LEADER: Ascribe to the Lord the glory due his name;

PEOPLE: Worship the Lord in the splendor of his holiness.

WOMEN: The voice of the Lord is over the waters;

MEN: The God of glory thunders,

PEOPLE: The Lord thunders over the mighty waters.

MEN: The voice of the Lord is powerful;

WOMEN: The voice of the Lord is majestic.

MEN: The voice of the Lord breaks the cedars;

WOMEN: The Lord breaks in pieces the cedars of Lebanon.

MEN: The voice of the Lord shakes the desert.

WOMEN: The voice of the Lord strikes with flashes of lightning.

MEN: The voice of the Lord shakes the desert;

WOMEN: The Lord shakes the Desert of Kadesh.

MEN: The voice of the Lord twists the oaks and strips the forests bare.

ALL: And in his temple all cry, "Glory!"

LEADER: The Lord sits enthroned over the flood;

PEOPLE: The Lord is enthroned as King forever.

LEADER: The Lord gives strength to his people;

PEOPLE: The Lord blesses his people with peace.

Script and/or Scripture arrangement from *The Psalms in Worship*, by Miller and Wyatt, © 1995. All rights reserved by Lillenas Publishing Company. Scripture quotes and paraphrases are from the *Holy Bible, New International Version®* (NIV®). Copyright © 1973, 1978, 1984 by International Bible Society. Used by permission of Zondervan Publishing House. All rights reserved.

Psalm 34

(vv. 1-8)

LEADER: I will extol the Lord at all times;

PEOPLE: His praise will always be on my lips.

LEADER: My soul will boast in the Lord;

PEOPLE: Let the afflicted hear and rejoice.

LEADER: Glorify the Lord with me;

PEOPLE: Let us exalt his name together.

SOLO: I sought the Lord, and he answered me; he delivered me from all my fears.

LEADER: Those who look to him are radiant;

PEOPLE: Their faces are never covered with shame.

SOLO: This poor man called, and the Lord heard him; he saved him out of all his troubles.

PEOPLE: The angel of the Lord encamps around those who fear him, and he delivers them.

LEADER: Taste and see that the Lord is good;

PEOPLE: Blessed is the man who takes refuge in him.

Script and/or Scripture arrangement from *The Psalms in Worship*, by Miller and Wyatt, © 1995. All rights reserved by Lillenas Publishing Company. Scripture quotes and paraphrases are from the *Holy Bible, New International Version*® (NIV®). Copyright © 1973, 1978, 1984 by International Bible Society. Used by permission of Zondervan Publishing House. All rights reserved.

Psalm 36

(vv. 5-9)

LEADER: Your love, O Lord, reaches to the heavens,

CHOIR: Your faithfulness to the skies, O Lord.

PEOPLE: How priceless is your unfailing love!

LEADER: Your righteousness is like the mighty mountains.

CHOIR: O Lord, your justice is like the great deep.

PEOPLE: How priceless is your unfailing love!

LEADER: O Lord, you preserve both man and beast.

CHOIR: Both high and low among men find refuge in the shadow of your wings.

PEOPLE: For with you is the fountain of life.

LEADER: They feast on the abundance of your house;

CHOIR: You give them drink from your river of delights.

PEOPLE: In your light, O Lord, we see light.

Script and/or Scripture arrangement from *The Psalms in Worship,* by Miller and Wyatt, © 1995. All rights reserved by Lillenas Publishing Company. Scripture quotes and paraphrases are from the *Holy Bible, New International Version*® (NIV®). Copyright © 1973, 1978, 1984 by International Bible Society. Used by permission of Zondervan Publishing House. All rights reserved.

Psalm 37

(vv. 1-11)

LEADER: Do not fret because of evil men or be envious of those who do wrong; for like the grass they will soon wither, like green plants they will soon die away.

MEN: Trust in the Lord and do good;

WOMEN: Dwell in the land and enjoy safe pasture.

LEADER: Delight yourself in the Lord and he will give you the desires of your heart.

ALL: Commit your way to the Lord;

LEADER: Trust in him and he will do this:

MEN: He will make your righteousness shine like the dawn.

WOMEN: He will make the justice of your cause like the noonday sun.

LEADER: Be still before the Lord and wait patiently for him.

ALL: Trust in the Lord.

LEADER: Do not fret when men succeed in their ways, when they carry out their wicked schemes.

MEN: Refrain from anger and turn from wrath;

WOMEN: Do not fret—it leads only to evil.

LEADER: For evil men will be cut off, but those who hope in the Lord will inherit the land. A little while, and the wicked will be no more; though you look for them, they will not be found.

ALL: But the meek will inherit the land and enjoy great peace.

Script and/or Scripture arrangement from *The Psalms in Worship,* by Miller and Wyatt, © 1995. All rights reserved by Lillenas Publishing Company. Scripture quotes and paraphrases are from the *Holy Bible, New International Version*® (NIV®). Copyright © 1973, 1978, 1984 by International Bible Society. Used by permission of Zondervan Publishing House. All rights reserved.

Psalm 38

Solo 1: O Lord, do not rebuke me in your anger or discipline me in your wrath.

Solo 2: For your arrows have pierced me, and your hand has come down upon me.

Solo 1: Because of your wrath there is no health in my body;

Solo 2: My bones have no soundness because of my sin.

Solo 1: My guilt has overwhelmed me like a burden too heavy to bear.

Solo 2: My wounds fester and are loathsome because of my sinful folly.

Solo 1: I am bowed down and brought very low;

Solo 2: All day long I go about mourning.

Solo 1: My back is filled with searing pain;

Solo 2: There is no health in my body.

Solo 1: I am feeble and utterly crushed;

Solo 2: I groan in anguish of heart.

Solo 1: All my longings lie open before you, O Lord;

Solo 2: My sighing is not hidden from you.

Solo 1: My heart pounds, my strength fails me;

Solo 2: Even the light has gone from my eyes.

Solo 1: My friends and companions avoid me because of my wounds;

Solo 2: My neighbors stay far away.

Solo 1: Those who seek my life set their traps, those who would harm me talk of my ruin;

Solo 2: All day long they plot deception.

Solo 1: I am like a deaf man, who cannot hear, like a mute, who cannot open his mouth;

Solo 2: I have become like a man who does not hear, whose mouth can offer no reply.

Solo 1: I wait for you, O Lord;

Solo 2: You will answer, O Lord my God.

Solo 1: For I said, "Do not let them gloat or exalt themselves over me when my foot slips."

Solo 2: For I am about to fall, and my pain is ever with me.

Solo 1: I confess my iniquity;

Solo 2: I am troubled by my sin.

Solo 1: Many are those who are my vigorous enemies; those who hate me without reason are numerous.

Solo 2: Those who repay my good with evil slander me when I pursue what is good.

Solo 1: O Lord, do not forsake me; be not far from me, O my God.

Solo 2: Come quickly to help me, O Lord my Savior.

Script and/or Scripture arrangement from *The Psalms in Worship,* by Miller and Wyatt, © 1995. All rights reserved by Lillenas Publishing Company. Scripture quotes and paraphrases are from the *Holy Bible, New International Version*® (NIV®). Copyright © 1973, 1978, 1984 by International Bible Society. Used by permission of Zondervan Publishing House. All rights reserved.

Psalm 39

SOLO 1: I said, "I will watch my ways and keep my tongue from sin."

SOLO 2: I said, "I will put a muzzle on my mouth as long as the wicked are in my presence."

SOLO 1: But when I was silent and still, not even saying anything good, my anguish increased.

SOLO 2: My heart grew hot within me, and as I meditated, the fire burned; then I spoke with my tongue: "Show me, O Lord, my life's end and the number of my days; let me know how fleeting is my life.

SOLO 1: "You have made my days a mere handbreadth;

SOLO 2: "The span of my years is as nothing before you.

ALL: "Each man's life is but a breath.

LEADER: "Man is a mere phantom as he goes to and fro:

RIGHT: "He bustles about, but only in vain;

LEFT: "He heaps up wealth, not knowing who will get it.

LEADER: "But now, Lord, what do I look for? My hope is in you.

RIGHT: "Save me from all my transgressions;

LEFT: "Do not make me the scorn of fools.

LEADER: "I was silent; I would not open my mouth, for you are the one who has done this.

RIGHT: "Remove your scourge from me;

LEFT: "I am overcome by the blow of your hand.

RIGHT: "You rebuke and discipline men for their sin;

LEFT: "You consume their wealth like a moth—

ALL: "Each man is but a breath.

SOLO 1: "Hear my prayer, O Lord, listen to my cry for help;

SOLO 2: "Be not deaf to my weeping.

SOLO 1: "For I dwell with you as an alien, a stranger, as all my fathers were.

SOLO 2: "Look away from me, that I may rejoice again before I depart and am no more."

Script and/or Scripture arrangement from *The Psalms in Worship*, by Miller and Wyatt, © 1995. All rights reserved by Lillenas Publishing Company. Scripture quotes and paraphrases are from the *Holy Bible, New International Version®* (NIV®). Copyright © 1973, 1978, 1984 by International Bible Society. Used by permission of Zondervan Publishing House. All rights reserved.

Psalm 40

(vv. 1-5, 7-16)

LEADER: I waited patiently for the Lord;

PEOPLE: He turned to me and heard my cry.

RIGHT: He lifted me out of the slimy pit.

LEFT: He lifted me out of the mud and mire;

RIGHT: He set my feet on a rock.

LEFT: He gave me a firm place to stand.

LEADER: He put a new song in my mouth, a hymn of praise to our God.

PEOPLE: Many will see and fear and put their trust in the Lord.

SOLO 1: Blessed is the man who makes the Lord his trust.

SOLO 2: Blessed is the man who does not look to the proud.

LEADER: Blessed is the man who does not look to those who turn aside to false gods.

PEOPLE: Many, O Lord my God, are the wonders you have done.

LEADER: The things you planned for us no one can recount to you.

PEOPLE: Many, O Lord my God, are the wonders you have done.

LEADER: Were I to speak and tell of them, they would be too many to declare.

PEOPLE: Many, O Lord my God, are the wonders you have done.

SOLO 1: Then I said, "Here I am, I have come—it is written about me in the scroll.

SOLO 2: "I desire to do your will, O my God; your law is within my heart."

RIGHT: I desire to do your will, O my God.

LEFT: Your law is within my heart.

SOLO 1: I proclaim righteousness in the great assembly;

SOLO 2: I do not seal my lips, as you know, O Lord.

RIGHT: I desire to do your will, O my God;

LEFT: Your law is within my heart.

Solo 2: I do not hide your righteousness in my heart;

Solo 1: I speak of your faithfulness and salvation.

Right: I desire to do your will, O my God;

Left: Your law is within my heart.

Leader: I do not conceal your love and your truth from the great assembly.

People: Do not withhold your mercy from me, O Lord.

Solo 1: O Lord, may your love and your truth always protect me.

Solo 2: For troubles without number surround me.

Right: Be pleased, O Lord, to save me;

Left: O Lord, come quickly to help me.

Solo 1: My sins have overtaken me, and I cannot see.

Solo 2: They are more than the hairs of my head, and my heart fails within me.

Right: Be pleased, O Lord, to save me;

Left: O Lord, come quickly to help me.

Leader: May all who seek to take my life be put to shame and confusion.

People: But may all who seek you rejoice and be glad in you.

Leader: May all who desire my ruin be turned back in disgrace.

People: But may all who seek you rejoice and be glad in you.

Leader: May those who say to me, "Aha! Aha!" be appalled at their own shame.

All: May those who love your salvation always say, "The Lord be exalted!"

Script and/or Scripture arrangement from *The Psalms in Worship*, by Miller and Wyatt, © 1995. All rights reserved by Lillenas Publishing Company. Scripture quotes and paraphrases are from the *Holy Bible, New International Version*® (NIV®). Copyright © 1973, 1978, 1984 by International Bible Society. Used by permission of Zondervan Publishing House. All rights reserved.

Psalm 42

LEADER: As the deer pants for streams of water, so my soul pants for you, O God.

SOLO 1: My soul thirsts for God, for the living God. When can I go and meet with God?

SOLO 2: My tears have been my food day and night, while men say to me all day long, "Where is your God?"

SOLO 3: These things I remember as I pour out my soul: how I used to go with the multitude, leading the procession to the house of God, with shouts of joy and thanksgiving among the festive throng.

LEADER: Why are you downcast, O my soul? Why so disturbed within me?

ALL: Put your hope in God, for I will yet praise him, my Savior and my God.

LEADER: Deep calls to deep in the roar of your waterfalls; all your waves and breakers have swept over me.

SOLO 3: By day the Lord directs his love, at night his song is with me—a prayer to the God of my life.

SOLO 1: I say to God my Rock, "Why have you forgotten me? Why must I go about mourning, oppressed by the enemy?"

SOLO 2: My bones suffer mortal agony as my foes taunt me, saying to me all day long, "Where is your God?"

LEADER: Why are you downcast, O my soul? Why so disturbed within me?

ALL: Put your hope in God, for I will yet praise him, my Savior and my God.

Script and/or Scripture arrangement from *The Psalms in Worship,* by Miller and Wyatt, © 1995. All rights reserved by Lillenas Publishing Company. Scripture quotes and paraphrases are from the *Holy Bible, New International Version*® (NIV®). Copyright © 1973, 1978, 1984 by International Bible Society. Used by permission of Zondervan Publishing House. All rights reserved.

Psalm 46

LEADER: God is our refuge and strength, an ever-present help in trouble.

ALL: Therefore we will not fear.

RIGHT: Though the earth give way . . .

LEFT: We will not fear.

RIGHT: Though the mountains fall into the heart of the sea . . .

LEFT: We will not fear.

LEADER: Though its waters roar and foam and the mountains quake with their surging . . .

ALL: We will not fear.

LEADER: There is a river whose streams make glad the city of God, the holy place where the Most High dwells.

RIGHT: God is within her, she will not fall;

LEFT: God will help her at break of day.

RIGHT: Nations are in uproar,

LEFT: Kingdoms fall;

RIGHT: He lifts his voice,

LEFT: The earth melts.

RIGHT: The Lord Almighty is with us;

LEFT: The God of Jacob is our fortress.

LEADER: Come and see the works of the Lord, the desolations he has brought on the earth.

PEOPLE: "Be still, and know that I am God."

LEADER: He makes wars cease to the ends of the earth; he breaks the bow and shatters the spear, he burns the shields with fire.

PEOPLE: "Be still, and know that I am God."

LEADER: "Be still, and know that I am God; I will be exalted among the nations, I will be exalted in the earth."

ALL: The Lord Almighty is with us; the God of Jacob is our fortress.

Script and/or Scripture arrangement from *The Psalms in Worship*, by Miller and Wyatt, © 1995. All rights reserved by Lillenas Publishing Company. Scripture quotes and paraphrases are from the *Holy Bible, New International Version*® (NIV®). Copyright © 1973, 1978, 1984 by International Bible Society. Used by permission of Zondervan Publishing House. All rights reserved.

Psalm 47

LEADER: How awesome is the Lord Most High, the great King over all the earth!

RIGHT: Clap your hands, all you nations;

LEFT: Shout to God with cries of joy.

LEADER: He subdued nations under us, peoples under our feet.

RIGHT: Clap your hands, all you nations;

LEFT: Shout to God with cries of joy.

LEADER: He chose our inheritance for us, the pride of Jacob, whom he loved.

RIGHT: Clap your hands, all you nations;

LEFT: Shout to God with cries of joy.

LEADER: God has ascended amid shouts of joy, the Lord amid the sounding of trumpets.

RIGHT: Sing praises to God,

ALL: Sing praises;

LEFT: Sing praises to our King,

ALL: Sing praises.

LEADER: For God is the King of all the earth;

PEOPLE: Sing to him a psalm of praise.

LEADER: God reigns over the nations;

PEOPLE: God is seated on his holy throne.

LEADER: The nobles of the nations assemble as the people of the God of Abraham, for the kings of the earth belong to God;

PEOPLE: He is greatly exalted.

Script and/or Scripture arrangement from *The Psalms in Worship*, by Miller and Wyatt, © 1995. All rights reserved by Lillenas Publishing Company. Scripture quotes and paraphrases are from the *Holy Bible, New International Version*® (NIV®). Copyright © 1973, 1978, 1984 by International Bible Society. Used by permission of Zondervan Publishing House. All rights reserved.

Psalm 49

Leader: Hear this, all you peoples; listen, all who live in this world, both low and high, rich and poor alike:

Solo 1: My mouth will speak words of wisdom; the utterance from my heart will give understanding.

Solo 2: I will turn my ear to a proverb; with the harp I will expound my riddle:

Solo 1: Why should I fear when evil days come, when wicked deceivers surround me—

Solo 2: Those who trust in their wealth and boast of their great riches?

Solo 1: No man can redeem the life of another or give to God a ransom for him—

Solo 2: The ransom for a life is costly, no payment is ever enough—that he should live on forever and not see decay.

Solo 1: For all can see that wise men die;

Solo 2: The foolish and the senseless alike perish and leave their wealth to others.

Solo 1: Their tombs will remain their houses forever,

Solo 2: Their dwellings will remain for endless generations, though they had named lands after themselves.

All: But man, despite his riches, does not endure; he is like the beasts that perish.

Leader: This is the fate of those who trust in themselves, and of their followers, who approve their sayings.

Solo 1: Like sheep they are destined for the grave, and death will feed on them.

Solo 2: The upright will rule over them in the morning; their forms will decay in the grave, far from their princely mansions.

Solo 1: But God will redeem my life from the grave;

Solo 2: He will surely take me to himself.

Solo 1: Do not be overawed when a man grows rich, when the splendor of his house increases;

Solo 2: For he will take nothing with him when he dies, his splendor will not descend with him.

SOLO 1: Though while he lived he counted himself blessed—

SOLO 2: And men praise you when you prosper—

SOLO 1: He will join the generation of his fathers,

SOLO 2: Who will never see the light of life.

ALL: A man who has riches without understanding is like the beasts that perish.

Script and/or Scripture arrangement from *The Psalms in Worship,* by Miller and Wyatt, © 1995. All rights reserved by Lillenas Publishing Company. Scripture quotes and paraphrases are from the *Holy Bible, New International Version*® (NIV®). Copyright © 1973, 1978, 1984 by International Bible Society. Used by permission of Zondervan Publishing House. All rights reserved.

Psalm 51

(vv. 1-17)

LEADER: A psalm of David. When the prophet Nathan came to him after David had committed adultery with Bathsheba.

CHOIR MEN: Have mercy on me, O God, according to your unfailing love;

CHOIR WOMEN: According to your great compassion blot out my transgressions.

SOLO 1: Wash away all my iniquity,

SOLO 2: Cleanse me from my sin.

SOLO 1: For I know my transgressions,

SOLO 2: My sin is always before me.

CHOIR MEN: Against you, you only, have I sinned and done what is evil in your sight,

CHOIR WOMEN: So that you are proved right when you speak and justified when you judge.

SOLO 1: Surely I was sinful at birth.

SOLO 2: Surely I was sinful from the time my mother conceived me.

SOLO 1: Surely you desire truth in the inner parts;

SOLO 2: You teach me wisdom in the inmost place.

CHOIR MEN: Cleanse me with hyssop, and I will be clean;

CHOIR WOMEN: Wash me, and I will be whiter than snow.

SOLO 1: Let me hear joy and gladness; let the bones you have crushed rejoice.

SOLO 2: Hide your face from my sins and blot out all my iniquity.

CHOIR MEN: Create in me a pure heart, O God.

CHOIR WOMEN: O God, renew a steadfast spirit within me.

SOLO 1: Do not cast me from your presence.

SOLO 2: Do not take your Holy Spirit from me.

SOLO 1: Restore to me the joy of your salvation and grant me a willing spirit, to sustain me.

SOLO 2: Then I will teach transgressors your ways, and sinners will turn back to you.

CHOIR MEN: Save me from bloodguilt, O God—

CHOIR WOMEN: O God, the God who saves me,

CHOIR MEN: And my tongue will sing of your righteousness.

CHOIR WOMEN: O God, the God who saves me.

SOLO 1: O Lord, open my lips, and my mouth will declare your praise.

SOLO 2: You do not delight in sacrifice, or I would bring it; you do not take pleasure in burnt offerings.

CHOIR MEN: The sacrifices of God are a broken spirit;

CHOIR WOMEN: A broken and contrite heart, O God, you will not despise.

Script and/or Scripture arrangement from *The Psalms in Worship,* by Miller and Wyatt, © 1995. All rights reserved by Lillenas Publishing Company. Scripture quotes and paraphrases are from the *Holy Bible, New International Version*® (NIV®). Copyright © 1973, 1978, 1984 by International Bible Society. Used by permission of Zondervan Publishing House. All rights reserved.

Psalm 53

LEADER: They are corrupt, and their ways are vile; there is no one who does good.

PEOPLE: The fool says in his heart, "There is no God."

LEADER: God looks down from heaven on the sons of men to see if there are any who understand, any who seek God.

PEOPLE: The fool says in his heart, "There is no God."

LEADER: Everyone has turned away, they have together become corrupt; there is no one who does good, not even one.

PEOPLE: The fool says in his heart, "There is no God."

LEADER: Will the evildoers never learn—those who devour my people as men eat bread and who do not call on God?

PEOPLE: The fool says in his heart, "There is no God."

LEADER: There they were, overwhelmed with dread, where there was nothing to dread. God scattered the bones of those who attacked you; you put them to shame, for God despised them.

PEOPLE: The fool says in his heart, "There is no God."

LEADER: Oh, that salvation for Israel would come out of Zion!

ALL: When God restores the fortunes of his people, let Jacob rejoice and Israel be glad!

Script and/or Scripture arrangement from *The Psalms in Worship,* by Miller and Wyatt, © 1995. All rights reserved by Lillenas Publishing Company. Scripture quotes and paraphrases are from the *Holy Bible, New International Version*® (NIV®). Copyright © 1973, 1978, 1984 by International Bible Society. Used by permission of Zondervan Publishing House. All rights reserved.

Psalm 56

Solo 1: Be merciful to me, O God, for men hotly pursue me; all day long they press their attack.

Solo 2: When I am afraid, I will trust in you.

Solo 1: My slanderers pursue me all day long; many are attacking me in their pride.

Solo 2: When I am afraid, I will trust in you.

Choir Women: In God, whose word I praise,

Choir Men: In God I trust;

Choir Women: I will not be afraid.

Choir Men: In God I trust.

Choir Women: What can mortal man do to me?

Choir Men: In God I trust.

Solo 1: All day long they twist my words; they are always plotting to harm me.

Solo 2: They conspire, they lurk, they watch my steps, eager to take my life.

Solo 1: On no account let them escape; in your anger, O God, bring down the nations.

Solo 2: Record my lament; list my tears on your scroll—are they not in your record?

Solo 1: Then my enemies will turn back when I call for help.

Solo 2: By this I will know that God is for me.

Choir Women: In God, whose word I praise,

Choir Men: In God I trust.

Choir Women: In the Lord, whose word I praise—

Choir Men: In God I trust.

Choir Women: I will not be afraid.

Choir Men: In God I trust.

Choir Women: What can man do to me?

Choir Men: In God I trust.

SOLO 1: I am under vows to you, O God; I will present my thank offerings to you.

SOLO 2: For you have delivered me from death and my feet from stumbling, that I may walk before God in the light of life.

Script and/or Scripture arrangement from *The Psalms in Worship,* by Miller and Wyatt, © 1995. All rights reserved by Lillenas Publishing Company. Scripture quotes and paraphrases are from the *Holy Bible, New International Version*® (NIV®). Copyright © 1973, 1978, 1984 by International Bible Society. Used by permission of Zondervan Publishing House. All rights reserved.

Psalm 57

LEADER: A psalm of David when he had fled from Saul into the cave.

RIGHT: Have mercy on me, O God,

LEFT: Have mercy on me, for in you my soul takes refuge.

LEADER: I will take refuge in the shadow of your wings until the disaster has passed.

RIGHT: I cry out to God Most High,

LEFT: To God, who fulfills his purpose for me.

RIGHT: He sends from heaven and saves me, rebuking those who hotly pursue me.

LEFT: God sends his love and his faithfulness.

LEADER: I am in the midst of lions; I lie among ravenous beasts—men whose teeth are spears and arrows, whose tongues are sharp swords.

RIGHT: Be exalted, O God, above the heavens.

LEFT: O God, let your glory be over all the earth.

LEADER: They spread a net for my feet—I was bowed down in distress. They dug a pit in my path—but they have fallen into it themselves.

RIGHT: My heart is steadfast, O God, my heart is steadfast;

LEFT: I will sing and make music.

RIGHT: Awake, my soul! Awake, harp and lyre!

LEFT: I will awaken the dawn.

LEADER: I will praise you, O Lord, among the nations.

PEOPLE: I will sing of you among the peoples.

LEADER: For great is your love, reaching to the heavens.

PEOPLE: Your faithfulness reaches to the skies.

LEADER: Be exalted, O God, above the heavens.

PEOPLE: O God, let your glory be over all the earth.

Script and/or Scripture arrangement from *The Psalms in Worship*, by Miller and Wyatt, © 1995. All rights reserved by Lillenas Publishing Company. Scripture quotes and paraphrases are from the *Holy Bible, New International Version*® (NIV®). Copyright © 1973, 1978, 1984 by International Bible Society. Used by permission of Zondervan Publishing House. All rights reserved.

Psalm 61

LEADER: Hear my cry, O God;

PEOPLE: Listen to my prayer.

LEADER: From the ends of the earth I call to you, I call as my heart grows faint;

PEOPLE: Lead me to the rock that is higher than I.

LEADER: For you have been my refuge, a strong tower against the foe.

PEOPLE: I long to dwell in your tent forever and take refuge in the shelter of your wings.

LEADER: For you have heard my vows, O God; you have given me the heritage of those who fear your name.

PEOPLE: Increase the days of the king's life, his years for many generations.

LEADER: May he be enthroned in God's presence forever; appoint your love and faithfulness to protect him.

PEOPLE: Then will I ever sing praise to your name and fulfill my vows day after day.

Script and/or Scripture arrangement from *The Psalms in Worship,* by Miller and Wyatt, © 1995. All rights reserved by Lillenas Publishing Company. Scripture quotes and paraphrases are from the *Holy Bible, New International Version*® (NIV®). Copyright © 1973, 1978, 1984 by International Bible Society. Used by permission of Zondervan Publishing House. All rights reserved.

Psalm 62

Solo 1: My soul finds rest in God alone;

All: My salvation comes from him.

Solo 1: He alone is my rock and my salvation;

All: He is my fortress, I will never be shaken.

Solo 1: How long will you assault a man? Would all of you throw him down— this leaning wall, this tottering fence?

Solo 2: They fully intend to topple him from his lofty place; they take delight in lies.

All: With their mouths they bless, but in their hearts they curse.

Solo 1: Find rest, O my soul, in God alone;

All: My hope comes from him.

Solo 2: He alone is my rock and my salvation;

All: He is my fortress, I will not be shaken.

Solo 1: My salvation and my honor depend on God;

All: He is my mighty rock, my refuge.

Solo 2: Trust in him at all times, O people; pour out your hearts to him,

All: For God is our refuge.

Solo 1: Lowborn men are but a breath, the highborn are but a lie;

Solo 2: If weighed on a balance, they are nothing;

All: Together they are only a breath.

Solo 1: Do not trust in extortion or take pride in stolen goods; though your riches increase, do not set your heart on them.

Solo 2: One thing God has spoken, two things have I heard: that you, O God, are strong, and that you, O Lord, are loving.

All: Surely you will reward each person according to what he has done.

Script and/or Scripture arrangement from *The Psalms in Worship*, by Miller and Wyatt, © 1995. All rights reserved by Lillenas Publishing Company. Scripture quotes and paraphrases are from the *Holy Bible, New International Version*® (NIV®). Copyright © 1973, 1978, 1984 by International Bible Society. Used by permission of Zondervan Publishing House. All rights reserved.

Psalm 63

Solo 1: O God, you are my God, earnestly I seek you;

Solo 2: My soul thirsts for you, my body longs for you, in a dry and weary land where there is no water.

Solo 1: I have seen you in the sanctuary and beheld your power and your glory.

Solo 2: Because your love is better than life, my lips will glorify you.

Solo 1: I will praise you as long as I live, and in your name I will lift up my hands.

Solo 2: My soul will be satisfied as with the richest of foods; with singing lips my mouth will praise you.

Solo 1: On my bed I remember you; I think of you through the watches of the night.

Solo 2: Because you are my help, I sing in the shadow of your wings.

Solo 1: My soul clings to you;

Solo 2: Your right hand upholds me.

Solo 1: They who seek my life will be destroyed;

Solo 2: They will go down to the depths of the earth.

Solo 1: They will be given over to the sword and become food for jackals. But the king will rejoice in God;

Solo 2: All who swear by God's name will praise him, while the mouths of liars will be silenced.

Script and/or Scripture arrangement from *The Psalms in Worship*, by Miller and Wyatt, © 1995. All rights reserved by Lillenas Publishing Company. Scripture quotes and paraphrases are from the *Holy Bible, New International Version*® (NIV®). Copyright © 1973, 1978, 1984 by International Bible Society. Used by permission of Zondervan Publishing House. All rights reserved.

Psalm 65

LEADER: Praise awaits you, O God, in Zion; to you our vows will be fulfilled.

PEOPLE: O you who hear prayer, to you all men will come.

LEADER: When we were overwhelmed by sins, you forgave our transgressions.

PEOPLE: Blessed are those you choose and bring near to live in your courts!

LEADER: We are filled with the good things of your house, of your holy temple.

RIGHT: You answer us with awesome deeds of righteousness, O God our Savior.

LEFT: You are the hope of all the ends of the earth and of the farthest seas,

RIGHT: Who formed the mountains by your power, having armed yourself with strength,

LEFT: Who stilled the roaring of the seas, the roaring of their waves, and the turmoil of the nations.

LEADER: Those living far away fear your wonders;

PEOPLE: Where morning dawns and evening fades you call forth songs of joy.

LEADER: You care for the land and water it;

PEOPLE: You enrich it abundantly.

LEADER: The streams of God are filled with water to provide the people with grain, for so you have ordained it.

RIGHT: You drench its furrows and level its ridges;

LEFT: You soften it with showers and bless its crops.

RIGHT: You crown the year with your bounty,

LEFT: And your carts overflow with abundance.

RIGHT: The grasslands of the desert overflow;

LEFT: The hills are clothed with gladness.

LEADER: The meadows are covered with flocks and the valleys are mantled with grain;

PEOPLE: They shout for joy and sing.

Script and/or Scripture arrangement from *The Psalms in Worship*, by Miller and Wyatt, © 1995. All rights reserved by Lillenas Publishing Company. Scripture quotes and paraphrases are from the *Holy Bible, New International Version*® (NIV®). Copyright © 1973, 1978, 1984 by International Bible Society. Used by permission of Zondervan Publishing House. All rights reserved.

Psalm 66

(vv. 1-4)

LEADER: Shout with joy

PEOPLE: Shout with joy to God.

ALL: Shout with joy to God, all the earth!

LEADER: Sing the glory of his name.

PEOPLE: Sing the glory of his name;

ALL: Make his praise glorious!

LEADER: Say to God, "How awesome are your deeds!"

PEOPLE: "How awesome are your deeds!"

LEADER: "So great is your power."

PEOPLE: "So great is your power."

ALL: "So great is your power that your enemies cringe before you.

LEADER: "All the earth bows down to you.

PEOPLE: "All the earth bows down to you; they sing praise to you,

ALL: "They sing praise to your name."

Script and/or Scripture arrangement from *The Psalms in Worship*, by Miller and Wyatt, © 1995. All rights reserved by Lillenas Publishing Company. Scripture quotes and paraphrases are from the *Holy Bible, New International Version*® (NIV®). Copyright © 1973, 1978, 1984 by International Bible Society. Used by permission of Zondervan Publishing House. All rights reserved.

Psalm 66

(vv. 5-6)

LEADER: A song for the director of music.

PEOPLE: Come and see what God has done,

SOLO: How awesome his works in man's behalf!

MEN: He turned the sea into dry land,

WOMEN: They passed through the waters on foot—

PEOPLE: Come, let us rejoice in him.

Script and/or Scripture arrangement from *The Psalms in Worship*, by Miller and Wyatt, © 1995. All rights reserved by Lillenas Publishing Company. Scripture quotes and paraphrases are from the *Holy Bible, New International Version®* (NIV®). Copyright © 1973, 1978, 1984 by International Bible Society. Used by permission of Zondervan Publishing House. All rights reserved.

Psalm 66

(vv. 8-10, 12)

LEADER: Praise our God, O peoples,

SOLO: Let the sound of his praise be heard;

PEOPLE: He has preserved our lives and kept our feet from slipping.

LEADER: For you, O God, tested us;

SOLO: You refined us like silver.

PEOPLE: You brought us to a place of abundance.

Script and/or Scripture arrangement from *The Psalms in Worship*, by Miller and Wyatt, © 1995. All rights reserved by Lillenas Publishing Company. Scripture quotes and paraphrases are from the *Holy Bible, New International Version®* (NIV®). Copyright © 1973, 1978, 1984 by International Bible Society. Used by permission of Zondervan Publishing House. All rights reserved.

Psalm 66

(vv. 16-20)

LEADER: Come and listen, all you who fear God;

PEOPLE: Let [us] tell you what he has done for [us].

SOLO: I cried out to him with my mouth;

LEADER: His praise was on my tongue.

PEOPLE: If [we] had cherished sin in [our] heart[s],

SOLO: The Lord would not have listened.

LEADER: But God has surely listened.

PEOPLE: God has surely listened and heard [our] voice[s] in prayer.

SOLO: Praise be to God.

LEADER: Praise be to God who has not rejected my prayer

PEOPLE: Praise be to God who has not rejected [our] prayer or withheld his love from [us]!

Script and/or Scripture arrangement from *The Psalms in Worship*, by Miller and Wyatt, © 1995. All rights reserved by Lillenas Publishing Company. Scripture quotes and paraphrases are from the *Holy Bible, New International Version*® (NIV®). Copyright © 1973, 1978, 1984 by International Bible Society. Used by permission of Zondervan Publishing House. All rights reserved.

Psalm 67

(vv. 1-7)

LEADER: May God be gracious to us and bless us and make his face shine upon us.

PEOPLE: This is our prayer, O God.

LEADER: That your ways may be known on earth, your salvation among all nations.

PEOPLE: Grant it to be, O God.

LEADER: May the peoples praise you, O God; may all the peoples praise you.

PEOPLE *(singing):* Praise God from whom all blessings flow. Praise Him all creatures here below.

LEADER: May the nations be glad and sing for joy, for you rule the peoples justly.

PEOPLE: We are glad, O God.

LEADER: May the peoples praise you, O God; may all the peoples praise you

PEOPLE *(singing):* Praise Him above ye heavenly hosts. Praise Father, Son, and Holy Ghost.

LEADER: Then the land will yield its harvest,

PEOPLE: And God, our God, will bless us.

Script and/or Scripture arrangement from *The Psalms in Worship*, by Miller and Wyatt, © 1995. All rights reserved by Lillenas Publishing Company. Scripture quotes and paraphrases are from the *Holy Bible, New International Version*® (NIV®). Copyright © 1973, 1978, 1984 by International Bible Society. Used by permission of Zondervan Publishing House. All rights reserved.

Psalm 71

(vv. 9-15, 17-24)

LEADER: Hear these words of a Jeremiah-like senior adult, speaking in the 71st psalm.

SOLO 1: Do not cast me away when I am old;

SOLO 2: Do not forsake me when my strength is gone.

SOLO 1: My enemies speak against me.

LEADER: They say, "God has forsaken him."

SOLO 1: Be not far from me, O God;

SOLO 2: Come quickly, O my God, to help me.

SOLO 1: As for me, I will always have hope;

LEADER: They say, "God has forsaken him; no one will rescue him."

SOLO 1: As for me, I will always have hope;

SOLO 2: I will praise you more and more.

SOLO 1: My mouth will tell of your righteousness.

LEADER: They say, "God has forsaken him; pursue him and seize him, for no one will rescue him."

SOLO 1: Since my youth, O God, you have taught me, and to this day I declare your marvelous deeds.

SOLO 2: Even when I am old and gray, do not forsake me, O God,

SOLO 1: Till I declare your power to the next generation,

SOLO 2: Your might to all who are to come.

LEADER: They say, "God has forsaken him."

SOLO 1: Your righteousness reaches to the skies, O God,

SOLO 2: You who have done great things.

SOLO 1: You will restore my life again.

SOLO 2: You will again bring me up.

SOLO 1: You will increase my honor and comfort me.

LEADER: They say, "No one will rescue him."

Solo 2: I will praise you with the harp for your faithfulness,

Solo 1: O my God;

Solo 2: I will sing praise to you with the lyre,

Solo 1: O Holy One of Israel.

Solo 2: My lips will shout for joy when I sing praise to you—

Solo 1: I, whom you have redeemed.

Solo 2: My tongue will tell of your righteous acts all day long,

Leader: Those who wanted to harm me have been put to shame and confusion.

All: You are my strong refuge!

Script and/or Scripture arrangement from *The Psalms in Worship,* by Miller and Wyatt, © 1995. All rights reserved by Lillenas Publishing Company. Scripture quotes and paraphrases are from the *Holy Bible, New International Version®* (NIV®). Copyright © 1973, 1978, 1984 by International Bible Society. Used by permission of Zondervan Publishing House. All rights reserved.

Psalm 73

Solo 1: But as for me, my feet had almost slipped; I had nearly lost my foothold.

Choir: Surely God is good to those who are pure in heart.

Solo 2: For I envied the arrogant when I saw the prosperity of the wicked.

Solo 1: They have no struggles;

Solo 2: Their bodies are healthy and strong.

Solo 1: They are free from the burdens common to man;

Solo 2: They are not plagued by human ills.

Choir Men: Surely in vain have I . . .

Choir Women: In vain have I . . .

Choir Men: Kept my heart pure . . .

Choir Women: In vain have I washed my hands in innocence.

Solo 1: Therefore pride is their necklace;

Solo 2: They clothe themselves with violence.

Solo 1: From their callous hearts comes iniquity;

Solo 2: The evil conceits of their minds know no limits.

Solo 1: They scoff, and speak with malice; in their arrogance they threaten oppression.

Solo 2: Their mouths lay claim to heaven, and their tongues take possession of the earth.

Choir Men: Surely in vain have I . . .

Choir Women: In vain have I . . .

Choir Men: Kept my heart pure . . .

Choir Women: In vain have I washed my hands in innocence.

Solo 1: Therefore their people turn to them and drink up waters in abundance.

Solo 2: They say, "How can God know? Does the Most High have knowledge?"

Solo 1: This is what the wicked are like—

Solo 2: Always carefree, they increase in wealth.

Choir Men: Surely in vain have I . . .

Choir Women: In vain have I . . .

Choir Men: Kept my heart pure . . .

Choir Women: In vain have I washed my hands in innocence.

Solo 1: All day long I have been plagued;

Solo 2: I have been punished every morning.

Solo 1: If I had said, "I will speak thus," I would have betrayed your children.

Solo 2: When I tried to understand all this, it was oppressive to me

Choir Men: Till I entered the sanctuary of God;

Choir Women: Then I understood their final destiny.

Solo 1: Surely you place them on slippery ground; you cast them down to ruin.

Solo 2: How suddenly are they destroyed, completely swept away by terrors!

Choir Men: As a dream when one awakes, so when you arise . . .

Choir Women: So when you arise, O Lord, you will despise them as fantasies.

Solo 1: When my heart was grieved and my spirit embittered, I was senseless and ignorant;

Solo 2: I was a brute beast before you.

Solo 1: Yet I am always with you; you hold me by my right hand.

Solo 2: You guide me with your counsel, and afterward you will take me into glory.

Solo 1: Whom have I in heaven but you?

Solo 2: And earth has nothing I desire besides you.

Choir Men: My flesh and my heart may fail,

Choir Women: But God is the strength of my heart.

Choir Men: My flesh and my heart may fail,

Choir Women: But God is my portion forever.

Solo 1: Those who are far from you will perish;

Solo 2: You destroy all who are unfaithful to you.

Solo 1: But as for me, it is good to be near God.

Solo 2: I have made the Sovereign Lord my refuge; I will tell of all your deeds.

Choir: Surely God is good to those who are pure in heart.

Script and/or Scripture arrangement from *The Psalms in Worship*, by Miller and Wyatt, © 1995. All rights reserved by Lillenas Publishing Company. Scripture quotes and paraphrases are from the *Holy Bible, New International Version*® (NIV®). Copyright © 1973, 1978, 1984 by International Bible Society. Used by permission of Zondervan Publishing House. All rights reserved.

Psalm 78

(vv. 1-4)

LEADER: O my people, hear my teaching;

PEOPLE: Listen to the words of my mouth.

LEADER: I will open my mouth in parables,

PEOPLE: I will utter hidden things, things from old.

LEADER: Things we have heard and known.

PEOPLE: Things our fathers have told us.

LEADER: We will not hide them from their children;

PEOPLE: We will tell the next generation the praiseworthy deeds of the Lord.

Script and/or Scripture arrangement from *The Psalms in Worship*, by Miller and Wyatt, © 1995. All rights reserved by Lillenas Publishing Company. Scripture quotes and paraphrases are from the *Holy Bible, New International Version*® (NIV®). Copyright © 1973, 1978, 1984 by International Bible Society. Used by permission of Zondervan Publishing House. All rights reserved.

Psalm 82

LEADER: God presides in the great assembly;

PEOPLE: He gives judgment among the "gods":

LEADER: "How long will you defend the unjust and show partiality to the wicked?

RIGHT: "Defend the cause of the weak and fatherless;

LEFT: "Maintain the rights of the poor and oppressed.

RIGHT: "Rescue the weak and needy.

LEFT: "Deliver them from the hand of the wicked.

RIGHT: "They know nothing.

LEFT: "They understand nothing.

RIGHT: "They walk about in darkness.

LEFT: "All the foundations of the earth are shaken.

LEADER: "I said, 'You are "gods"; you are all sons of the Most High.' But you will die like mere men; you will fall like every other ruler."

PEOPLE: Rise up, O God, judge the earth, for all the nations are your inheritance.

Script and/or Scripture arrangement from *The Psalms in Worship,* by Miller and Wyatt, © 1995. All rights reserved by Lillenas Publishing Company. Scripture quotes and paraphrases are from the *Holy Bible, New International Version*® (NIV®). Copyright © 1973, 1978, 1984 by International Bible Society. Used by permission of Zondervan Publishing House. All rights reserved.

Psalm 84

(vv. 1-4, 10-12)

LEADER: My soul yearns, even faints, for the courts of the Lord.

PEOPLE: How lovely is your dwelling place, O Lord Almighty!

LEADER: My heart and my flesh cry out for the living God.

PEOPLE: How lovely is your dwelling place, O Lord Almighty!

LEADER: Even the sparrow has found a home, and the swallow a nest for herself, where she may have her young—a place near your altar, O Lord Almighty, my King and my God.

PEOPLE: Blessed are those who dwell in your house; they are ever praising you.

LEADER: Better is one day in your courts than a thousand elsewhere.

PEOPLE: For the Lord God is a sun and shield.

LEADER: I would rather be a doorkeeper in the house of my God than dwell in the tents of the wicked.

PEOPLE: The Lord bestows favor and honor;

LEADER: No good thing does he withhold from those whose walk is blameless.

PEOPLE: O Lord Almighty, blessed is the man who trusts in you.

Script and/or Scripture arrangement from *The Psalms in Worship,* by Miller and Wyatt, © 1995. All rights reserved by Lillenas Publishing Company. Scripture quotes and paraphrases are from the *Holy Bible, New International Version*® (NIV®). Copyright © 1973, 1978, 1984 by International Bible Society. Used by permission of Zondervan Publishing House. All rights reserved.

Psalm 86

SOLO 1: Hear, O Lord, and answer me, for I am poor and needy.

SOLO 2: Guard my life, for I am devoted to you. You are my God; save your servant who trusts in you.

SOLO 1: Have mercy on me, O Lord, for I call to you all day long.

SOLO 2: Bring joy to your servant, for to you, O Lord, I lift up my soul.

CHOIR: You are forgiving and good, O Lord, abounding in love to all who call to you.

SOLO 1: Hear my prayer, O Lord; listen to my cry for mercy.

SOLO 2: In the day of my trouble I will call to you, for you will answer me.

SOLO 1: Among the gods there is none like you, O Lord; no deeds can compare with yours.

SOLO 2: All the nations you have made will come and worship before you, O Lord; they will bring glory to your name.

CHOIR: For you are great and do marvelous deeds; you alone are God.

SOLO 1: Teach me your way, O Lord, and I will walk in your truth; give me an undivided heart, that I may fear your name.

SOLO 2: I will praise you, O Lord my God, with all my heart; I will glorify your name forever.

SOLO 1: For great is your love toward me; you have delivered me from the depths of the grave.

SOLO 2: The arrogant are attacking me, O God; a band of ruthless men seeks my life—men without regard for you.

CHOIR: But you, O Lord, are a compassionate and gracious God, slow to anger, abounding in love and faithfulness.

SOLO 1: Turn to me and have mercy on me; grant your strength to your servant and save the son of your maidservant.

SOLO 2: Give me a sign of your goodness, that my enemies may see it and be put to shame, for you, O Lord, have helped me and comforted me.

Script and/or Scripture arrangement from *The Psalms in Worship,* by Miller and Wyatt, © 1995. All rights reserved by Lillenas Publishing Company. Scripture quotes and paraphrases are from the *Holy Bible, New International Version*® (NIV®). Copyright © 1973, 1978, 1984 by International Bible Society. Used by permission of Zondervan Publishing House. All rights reserved.

Psalm 88

Solo 1: May my prayer come before you; turn your ear to my cry.

Solo 2: For my soul is full of trouble and my life draws near the grave.

All: O Lord, the God who saves me, day and night I cry out before you.

Solo 1: I am counted among those who go down to the pit; I am like a man without strength.

Solo 2: I am set apart with the dead, like the slain who lie in the grave, whom you remember no more, who are cut off from your care.

All: O Lord, the God who saves me, day and night I cry out before you.

Solo 1: You have put me in the lowest pit, in the darkest depths.

Solo 2: Your wrath lies heavily upon me; you have overwhelmed me with all your waves.

All: O Lord, the God who saves me, day and night I cry out before you.

Solo 1: You have taken from me my closest friends and have made me repulsive to them.

Solo 2: I am confined and cannot escape; my eyes are dim with grief.

All: O Lord, the God who saves me, day and night I cry out before you.

Solo 1: Do you show your wonders to the dead?

Solo 2: Do those who are dead rise up and praise you?

All: I call to you, O Lord, every day; I spread out my hands to you.

Solo 1: Is your love declared in the grave?

Solo 2: Is your faithfulness in Destruction?

All: I call to you, O Lord, every day; I spread out my hands to you.

Solo 1: Are your wonders known in the place of darkness?

Solo 2: Are your righteous deeds known in the land of oblivion?

All: I call to you, O Lord, every day; I spread out my hands to you.

Solo 1: In the morning my prayer comes before you.

Solo 2: Why, O Lord, do you reject me and hide your face from me?

All: But I cry to you for help, O Lord.

SOLO 1: From my youth I have been afflicted and close to death;

SOLO 2: I have suffered your terrors and am in despair.

ALL: But I cry to you for help, O Lord.

SOLO 1: Your wrath has swept over me;

SOLO 2: Your terrors have destroyed me.

ALL: But I cry to you for help, O Lord.

SOLO 1: All day long they surround me like a flood;

SOLO 2: They have completely engulfed me.

ALL: But I cry to you for help, O Lord.

SOLO 1: You have taken my companions and loved ones from me;

SOLO 2: The darkness is my closest friend.

ALL: But I cry to you for help, O Lord.

Script and/or Scripture arrangement from *The Psalms in Worship*, by Miller and Wyatt, © 1995. All rights reserved by Lillenas Publishing Company. Scripture quotes and paraphrases are from the *Holy Bible, New International Version*® (NIV®). Copyright © 1973, 1978, 1984 by International Bible Society. Used by permission of Zondervan Publishing House. All rights reserved.

Psalm 89

(vv. 5-18)

Solo 1: The heavens praise your wonders, O Lord, your faithfulness too, in the assembly of the holy ones.

Choir Women: For who in the skies above can compare with the Lord?

Choir Men: Who is like the Lord among the heavenly beings?

Solo 2: In the council of the holy ones God is greatly feared; he is more awesome than all who surround him.

Choir Women: O Lord God Almighty, who is like you?

Choir Men: You are mighty, O Lord, and your faithfulness surrounds you.

Solo 1: You rule over the surging sea; when its waves mount up, you still them.

Solo 2: You crushed Rahab like one of the slain; with your strong arm you scattered your enemies.

Choir Women: The heavens are yours, and yours also the earth;

Choir Men: You founded the world and all that is in it.

Solo 1: You created the north and the south; Tabor and Hermon sing for joy at your name.

Choir Women: Your arm is endued with power;

Choir Men: Your hand is strong, your right hand exalted.

Choir Women: Righteousness and justice are the foundation of your throne;

Choir Men: Love and faithfulness go before you.

Solo 2: Blessed are those who have learned to acclaim you, who walk in the light of your presence, O Lord.

Choir Women: They rejoice in your name all day long.

Choir Men: They exult in your righteousness.

Solo 1: For you are their glory and strength, and by your favor you exalt our horn.

Solo 2: Indeed, our shield belongs to the Lord, our king to the Holy One of Israel.

Script and/or Scripture arrangement from *The Psalms in Worship*, by Miller and Wyatt, © 1995. All rights reserved by Lillenas Publishing Company. Scripture quotes and paraphrases are from the *Holy Bible, New International Version*® (NIV®). Copyright © 1973, 1978, 1984 by International Bible Society. Used by permission of Zondervan Publishing House. All rights reserved.

Psalm 90

(vv. 1-4, 7-8, 10, 12, 17)

LEADER: Traditionally, Psalm 90 has been ascribed to Moses, which makes this the most ancient song in the Psalter. Can you see him? A road-weary Moses alone with God in a shelter somewhere on the backside of a desert.

SOLO 1: Lord, you have been our dwelling place throughout all generations. Before the mountains were born or you brought forth the earth and the world, from everlasting to everlasting...

SOLO 2: From everlasting to everlasting.

SOLO 1: From everlasting to everlasting you are God.

LEADER: Psalm 90 contrasts God's eternal nature with our frailty.

SOLO 1: Lord, you turn men back to dust, saying,

SOLO 2: "Return to dust, O sons of men."

SOLO 1: For a thousand years in your sight are like a day that has just gone by,

SOLO 2: Or like a watch in the night.

LEADER: Moses reminds us that a thousand years are like a day to God. He is not limited by the time that ticks on our clocks.

SOLO 1: Lord, we are consumed by your anger and terrified by your indignation.

SOLO 2: You have set our iniquities before you, our secret sins in the light of your presence.

SOLO 1: The length of our days is seventy years—or eighty if we have the strength; yet their span is but trouble and sorrow

SOLO 2: For they quickly pass, and we fly away.

LEADER: Who should better know of the brevity of time than Moses? How often did he remove himself from the crowd to discuss God's time table.

SOLO 1: Lord, teach us to number our days aright, that we may gain a heart of wisdom.

SOLO 2: May the favor of the Lord rest upon us;

SOLO 1: Establish the work of our hands for us—

ALL: Yes, establish the work of our hands.

Script and/or Scripture arrangement from *The Psalms in Worship*, by Miller and Wyatt, © 1995. All rights reserved by Lillenas Publishing Company. Scripture quotes and paraphrases are from the *Holy Bible, New International Version*® (NIV®). Copyright © 1973, 1978, 1984 by International Bible Society. Used by permission of Zondervan Publishing House. All rights reserved.

Psalm 93

LEADER: The Lord reigns, he is robed in majesty;

CHOIR: The Lord is robed in majesty.

PEOPLE: The Lord is armed with strength.

LEADER: The world is firmly established; it cannot be moved.

CHOIR: Your throne was established long ago, O Lord.

PEOPLE: O Lord, you are from all eternity.

LEADER: The seas have lifted up, O Lord;

CHOIR: The seas have lifted up their voice;

PEOPLE: The seas have lifted up their pounding waves.

LEADER: Mightier than the thunder of the great waters,

CHOIR: Mightier than the breakers of the sea—

PEOPLE: The Lord on high is mighty.

LEADER: O Lord, your statutes stand firm.

CHOIR: For endless days, O Lord, your statutes stand firm.

PEOPLE: Holiness adorns your house for endless days, O Lord.

Script and/or Scripture arrangement from *The Psalms in Worship*, by Miller and Wyatt, © 1995. All rights reserved by Lillenas Publishing Company. Scripture quotes and paraphrases are from the *Holy Bible, New International Version*® (NIV®). Copyright © 1973, 1978, 1984 by International Bible Society. Used by permission of Zondervan Publishing House. All rights reserved.

Psalm 95

(vv. 1-7)

LEADER: Come, let us sing for joy to the Lord.

PEOPLE: Come, let us shout aloud to the Rock of our salvation.

LEADER: Let us come before him with thanksgiving.

PEOPLE: Let us extol him with music and song.

LEADER: For the Lord is the great God.

PEOPLE: The Lord is the great King above all gods.

LEADER: In his hand are the depths of the earth, and the mountain peaks belong to him.

PEOPLE: The sea is his, for he made it, and his hands formed the dry land.

LEADER: Come, let us bow down in worship,

PEOPLE: Come, let us kneel before the Lord our Maker.

LEADER: For he is our God

PEOPLE: And we are the people of his pasture, the flock under his care.

Script and/or Scripture arrangement from *The Psalms in Worship,* by Miller and Wyatt, © 1995. All rights reserved by Lillenas Publishing Company. Scripture quotes and paraphrases are from the *Holy Bible, New International Version*® (NIV®). Copyright © 1973, 1978, 1984 by International Bible Society. Used by permission of Zondervan Publishing House. All rights reserved.

Psalm 97

(vv. 1-6)

LEADER: Hear a song about our awesome God.

ALL: The Lord reigns,

WOMEN: Let the earth be glad;

MEN: Let distant shores rejoice.

CHOIR: Clouds and thick darkness surround him;

MEN: Righteousness and justice are the foundation of his throne.

WOMEN: Fire goes before him.

CHOIR: His lightning lights up the world;

MEN: The earth sees and trembles.

WOMEN: The mountains melt like wax before the Lord,

CHOIR: Before the Lord of all the earth.

LEADER: The heavens proclaim his righteousness,

ALL: And all the peoples see his glory.

Script and/or Scripture arrangement from *The Psalms in Worship*, by Miller and Wyatt, © 1995. All rights reserved by Lillenas Publishing Company. Scripture quotes and paraphrases are from the *Holy Bible, New International Version*® (NIV®). Copyright © 1973, 1978, 1984 by International Bible Society. Used by permission of Zondervan Publishing House. All rights reserved.

Psalm 100

LEADER: Shout for joy to the Lord, all the earth.

CHOIR: Worship the Lord with gladness;

PEOPLE: Come before the Lord with joyful songs.

LEADER: Know that the Lord is God.

CHOIR: It is he who made us, and we are his;

MEN: We are his people.

WOMAN: We are the sheep of his pasture.

LEADER: Enter his gates with thanksgiving.

CHOIR: Enter his courts with praise;

MEN: Give thanks to him and praise his name.

WOMEN: Give thanks to him, for the Lord is good.

CHOIR: Give thanks to him, for his love endures forever;

PEOPLE: His faithfulness continues through all generations.

Script and/or Scripture arrangement from *The Psalms in Worship*, by Miller and Wyatt, © 1995. All rights reserved by Lillenas Publishing Company. Scripture quotes and paraphrases are from the *Holy Bible, New International Version*® (NIV®). Copyright © 1973, 1978, 1984 by International Bible Society. Used by permission of Zondervan Publishing House. All rights reserved.

Psalm 103

(vv. 1-5, 20-22)

LEADER: Praise the Lord, O my soul;

PEOPLE: All my inmost being, praise his holy name.

LEADER: Praise the Lord, O my soul,

PEOPLE: And forget not all his benefits.

LEADER: Praise the Lord,

PEOPLE: Who forgives all your sins.

LEADER: Praise the Lord,

PEOPLE: Who heals all your diseases.

LEADER: Praise the Lord,

PEOPLE: Who redeems your life from the pit and crowns you with love and compassion.

LEADER: Praise the Lord,

PEOPLE: Who satisfies your desires with good things so that your youth is renewed like the eagle's.

LEADER: Praise the Lord, you his angels.

PEOPLE: Praise the Lord, you mighty ones who do his bidding.

LEADER: Praise the Lord, you who obey his word.

PEOPLE: Praise the Lord, all his heavenly hosts.

LEADER: Praise the Lord, you his servants who do his will.

PEOPLE: Praise the Lord, all his works everywhere in his dominion.

ALL: Praise the Lord, O my soul.

Script and/or Scripture arrangement from *The Psalms in Worship,* by Miller and Wyatt, © 1995. All rights reserved by Lillenas Publishing Company. Scripture quotes and paraphrases are from the *Holy Bible, New International Version*® (NIV®). Copyright © 1973, 1978, 1984 by International Bible Society. Used by permission of Zondervan Publishing House. All rights reserved.

Psalm 103

(vv. 8-18)

LEADER: The Lord is compassionate and gracious, slow to anger, abounding in love.

PEOPLE: He will not always accuse, nor will he harbor his anger forever.

LEADER: The Lord does not treat us as our sins deserve

PEOPLE: Or repay us according to our iniquities.

LEADER: For as high as the heavens are above the earth,

PEOPLE: So great is his love for those who fear him;

LEADER: As far as the east is from the west,

PEOPLE: So far has he removed our transgressions from us.

LEADER: As a father has compassion on his children,

PEOPLE: So the Lord has compassion on those who fear him.

LEADER: The Lord knows how we are formed.

PEOPLE: The Lord remembers that we are dust.

LEADER: As for man, his days are like grass,

PEOPLE: He flourishes like a flower of the field;

LEADER: The wind blows over it and it is gone,

PEOPLE: And its place remembers it no more.

LEADER: But from everlasting to everlasting the Lord's love is with those who fear him,

PEOPLE: And his righteousness with their children's children—

LEADER: With those who keep his covenant

PEOPLE: And remember to obey his precepts.

Script and/or Scripture arrangement from *The Psalms in Worship*, by Miller and Wyatt, © 1995. All rights reserved by Lillenas Publishing Company. Scripture quotes and paraphrases are from the *Holy Bible, New International Version*® (NIV®). Copyright © 1973, 1978, 1984 by International Bible Society. Used by permission of Zondervan Publishing House. All rights reserved.

Psalm 107

(v. 1)

LEADER: The 107th psalm tells us to, "Give thanks."

PEOPLE: "Give thanks" to whom?

LEADER: Give thanks to the Lord.

PEOPLE: "Give thanks to the Lord" for what reason?

LEADER: Give thanks to the Lord, for he is good.

PEOPLE: "Give thanks to the Lord, for he is good"; why?

LEADER: Give thanks to the Lord, for he is good; his love endures.

PEOPLE: "Give thanks to the Lord, for he is good; his love endures" for how long?

LEADER: Give thanks to the Lord, for he is good; his love endures forever.

PEOPLE: We "give thanks to the Lord, for he is good; his love endures forever."

Script and/or Scripture arrangement from *The Psalms in Worship*, by Miller and Wyatt, © 1995. All rights reserved by Lillenas Publishing Company. Scripture quotes and paraphrases are from the *Holy Bible, New International Version*® (NIV®). Copyright © 1973, 1978, 1984 by International Bible Society. Used by permission of Zondervan Publishing House. All rights reserved.

Psalm 107

(vv. 2-11, 13-15, 22, 42-43)

LEADER: Let the redeemed of the Lord say

CHOIR: We are the redeemed!

LEADER: Those he redeemed from the hand of the foe,

CHOIR: We are the redeemed!

LEADER: Those he gathered from east and west,

CHOIR: We are the redeemed!

[All sing "Redeemed, How I Love to Proclaim It," or similar.]

LEADER: Some [he redeemed] wandered in the desert wastelands, finding no way to a city where they could settle.

SOLO 1: They were hungry and thirsty, and their lives ebbed away.

LEADER: Then they cried out to the Lord in their trouble,

SOLO 2: And God delivered them from their distress.

SOLO 1: He led them by a straight way to a city where they could settle.

LEADER: Let them give thanks to the Lord for his unfailing love and his wonderful deeds,

SOLO 1: For he satisfies the thirsty

SOLO 2: And fills the hungry with good things.

LEADER: Some sat in darkness and the deepest gloom,

SOLO 1: Prisoners suffering in iron chains,

SOLO 2: For they had rebelled against the words of God and despised the counsel of the Most High.

LEADER: Then they cried to the Lord in their trouble, and he saved them from their distress.

SOLO 1: He brought them out of darkness and the deepest gloom.

SOLO 2: He broke away their chains.

SOLO 1: Let them give thanks to the Lord for his unfailing love

SOLO 2: And his wonderful deeds for men.

SOLO 1: Let them sacrifice thank offerings

SOLO 2: And tell of his works with songs of joy.

[All sing "Joyful, Joyful, We Adore Thee," or similar.]

LEADER: Let the redeemed of the Lord say

CHOIR: We are redeemed!

LEADER: [The redeemed] see and rejoice.

ALL: Let the redeemed heed these things and consider the great love of the Lord.

Script and/or Scripture arrangement from *The Psalms in Worship,* by Miller and Wyatt, © 1995. All rights reserved by Lillenas Publishing Company. Scripture quotes and paraphrases are from the *Holy Bible, New International Version*® (NIV®). Copyright © 1973, 1978, 1984 by International Bible Society. Used by permission of Zondervan Publishing House. All rights reserved.

Psalm 110

LEADER: The Lord says to my Lord:

ALL: "Sit at my right hand until I make your enemies a footstool for your feet."

LEADER: The Lord will extend your mighty scepter from Zion; you will rule in the midst of your enemies.

MEN: Your troops will be willing on your day of battle.

WOMEN: Arrayed in holy majesty,

MEN: From the womb of the dawn

WOMEN: You will receive the dew of your youth.

LEADER: The Lord has sworn and will not change his mind:

MEN: "You are a priest forever,

WOMEN: "In the order of Melchizedek."

LEADER: The Lord is at your right hand;

MEN: He will crush kings on the day of his wrath.

WOMEN: He will judge the nations,

MEN: Heaping up the dead and crushing the rulers of the whole earth.

WOMEN: He will drink from a brook beside the way;

ALL: Therefore he will lift up his head.

Script and/or Scripture arrangement from *The Psalms in Worship*, by Miller and Wyatt, © 1995. All rights reserved by Lillenas Publishing Company. Scripture quotes and paraphrases are from the *Holy Bible, New International Version*® (NIV®). Copyright © 1973, 1978, 1984 by International Bible Society. Used by permission of Zondervan Publishing House. All rights reserved.

Psalm 111

LEADER: A psalm reminding us that everything God does is good.

ALL: Praise the Lord.

LEADER: I will extol the Lord with all my heart in the council of the upright and in the assembly.

ALL: Great are the works of the Lord;

MEN: They are pondered by all who delight in them.

ALL: Glorious and majestic are his deeds,

WOMEN: And his righteousness endures forever.

LEADER: He has caused his wonders to be remembered;

ALL: The Lord is gracious and compassionate.

MEN: He provides food for those who fear him;

ALL: He remembers his covenant forever.

LEADER: He has shown his people the power of his works,

ALL: Giving them the lands of other nations.

WOMEN: The works of his hands are faithful and just;

ALL: All of his precepts are trustworthy.

MEN: They are steadfast for ever and ever, done in faithfulness and uprightness.

LEADER: He provided redemption for his people;

ALL: He ordained his covenant forever—holy and awesome is his name.

LEADER: The fear of the Lord is the beginning of wisdom;

WOMEN: All who follow his precepts have good understanding.

ALL: To him belongs eternal praise.

Script and/or Scripture arrangement from *The Psalms in Worship*, by Miller and Wyatt, © 1995. All rights reserved by Lillenas Publishing Company. Scripture quotes and paraphrases are from the *Holy Bible, New International Version*® (NIV®). Copyright © 1973, 1978, 1984 by International Bible Society. Used by permission of Zondervan Publishing House. All rights reserved.

Psalm 112

(vv. 1-9)

LEADER: A psalm reminding us that faith in God is following His commands.

ALL: Praise the Lord.

LEADER: Blessed is the man who fears the Lord.

ALL: Blessed is the man who finds great delight in his commands.

LEADER: His children will be mighty in the land;

MEN: The generation of the upright will be blessed.

LEADER: Wealth and riches are in his house,

WOMEN: And his righteousness endures forever.

LEADER: Even in darkness light dawns for the upright,

ALL: For the gracious and compassionate and righteous man.

LEADER: Good will come to him who is generous and lends freely,

ALL: Who conducts his affairs with justice.

LEADER: Surely he will never be shaken;

ALL: A righteous man will be remembered forever.

LEADER: He will have no fear of bad news;

MEN: His heart is steadfast, trusting in the Lord.

LEADER: His heart is secure, he will have no fear;

WOMEN: In the end he will look in triumph on his foes.

LEADER: He has scattered abroad his gifts to the poor,

ALL: His righteousness endures forever.

Script and/or Scripture arrangement from *The Psalms in Worship*, by Miller and Wyatt, © 1995. All rights reserved by Lillenas Publishing Company. Scripture quotes and paraphrases are from the *Holy Bible, New International Version*® (NIV®). Copyright © 1973, 1978, 1984 by International Bible Society. Used by permission of Zondervan Publishing House. All rights reserved.

Psalm 113

(vv. 1-8)

LEADER: A psalm reminding us of the breadth of God's care and mercy.

ALL: Praise the Lord.

LEADER: Praise, O servants of the Lord,

ALL: Praise the name of the Lord.

LEADER: Let the name of the Lord be praised,

ALL: Both now and forevermore.

LEADER: From the rising of the sun to the place where it sets,

ALL: The name of the Lord is to be praised.

LEADER: The Lord is exalted over all the nations,

WOMEN: His glory above the heavens.

LEADER: Who is like the Lord our God, the one who sits enthroned on high.

MEN: The One who stoops down to look on the heavens and the earth?

LEADER: He raises the poor from the dust and lifts the needy from the ash heap;

WOMEN: He seats them with princes.

MEN: He seats them with the princes of their people.

ALL: Praise the Lord.

Script and/or Scripture arrangement from *The Psalms in Worship*, by Miller and Wyatt, © 1995. All rights reserved by Lillenas Publishing Company. Scripture quotes and paraphrases are from the *Holy Bible, New International Version*® (NIV®). Copyright © 1973, 1978, 1984 by International Bible Society. Used by permission of Zondervan Publishing House. All rights reserved.

Psalm 115

LEADER: Not to us, O Lord, not to us but to your name be the glory, because of your love and faithfulness.

PEOPLE: Why do the nations say, "Where is their God?"

LEADER: Our God is in heaven; he does whatever pleases him.

PEOPLE: But their idols are silver and gold, made by the hands of men.

RIGHT: They have mouths, but cannot speak.

LEFT: They have eyes, but cannot see.

RIGHT: They have ears, but cannot hear.

LEFT: They have noses, but cannot smell.

RIGHT: They have hands, but cannot feel.

LEFT: They have feet, but cannot walk; nor can they utter a sound with their throats.

ALL: Those who make them will be like them, and so will all who trust in them.

LEADER: O house of Israel, trust in the Lord—

PEOPLE: He is their help and shield.

LEADER: O house of Aaron, trust in the Lord—

PEOPLE: He is their help and shield.

LEADER: You who fear him, trust in the Lord—

PEOPLE: He is their help and shield.

LEADER: The Lord remembers us and will bless us:

RIGHT: He will bless the house of Israel,

LEFT: He will bless the house of Aaron,

ALL: He will bless those who fear the Lord—small and great alike.

LEADER: May the Lord make you increase, both you and your children.

PEOPLE: Our God is in heaven; he does whatever pleases him.

LEADER: May you be blessed by the Lord, the Maker of heaven and earth.

PEOPLE: The Lord is our help and shield.

LEADER: The highest heavens belong to the Lord, but the earth he has given to man.

PEOPLE: The Lord remembers us and will bless us:

LEADER: It is not the dead who praise the Lord, those who go down to silence;

PEOPLE: It is we who extol the Lord, both now and forevermore.

ALL: Praise the Lord.

Script and/or Scripture arrangement from *The Psalms in Worship*, by Miller and Wyatt, © 1995. All rights reserved by Lillenas Publishing Company. Scripture quotes and paraphrases are from the *Holy Bible, New International Version*® (NIV®). Copyright © 1973, 1978, 1984 by International Bible Society. Used by permission of Zondervan Publishing House. All rights reserved.

Psalm 117

LEADER: Praise the Lord, all you nations.

PEOPLE: Praise the Lord!

LEADER: Extol him, all you peoples.

PEOPLE: Praise the Lord!

LEADER: For great is his love toward us.

PEOPLE: Praise the Lord!

LEADER: The faithfulness of the Lord endures forever.

PEOPLE: Praise the Lord!

Script and/or Scripture arrangement from *The Psalms in Worship*, by Miller and Wyatt, © 1995. All rights reserved by Lillenas Publishing Company. Scripture quotes and paraphrases are from the *Holy Bible, New International Version*® (NIV®). Copyright © 1973, 1978, 1984 by International Bible Society. Used by permission of Zondervan Publishing House. All rights reserved.

Psalm 118

LEADER: Give thanks to the Lord, for he is good;

CHOIR: His love endures forever.

LEADER: Let Israel say:

CHOIR: "His love endures forever."

LEADER: Let the house of Aaron say:

CHOIR: "His love endures forever."

LEADER: Let those who fear the Lord say:

CHOIR: "His love endures forever."

TESTIMONY 1: In my anguish I cried to the Lord, and he answered by setting me free. The Lord is with me; I will not be afraid. What can man do to me? The Lord is with me; he is my helper. I will look in triumph on my enemies.

LEADER: It is better to take refuge in the Lord than to trust in man. It is better to take refuge in the Lord than to trust in princes.

CHOIR: "His love endures forever."

TESTIMONY 2: All the nations surrounded me. They surrounded me on every side. They swarmed around me like bees, but they died out as quickly as burning thorns; in the name of the Lord I cut them off.

LEADER: I was pushed back and about to fall, but the Lord helped me. The Lord is my strength and my song; he has become my salvation.

CHOIR: "His love endures forever."

TESTIMONY 3: Shouts of joy and victory resound in the tents of the righteous: "The Lord's right hand has done mighty things! The Lord's right hand is lifted high."

LEADER: I will not die but live, and will proclaim what the Lord has done. The Lord has chastened me severely, but he has not given me over to death.

CHOIR: "His love endures forever."

TESTIMONY 4: Open for me the gates of righteousness; I will enter and give thanks to the Lord. This is the gate of the Lord through which the righteous may enter. I will give you thanks, for you answered me; you have become my salvation.

LEADER: The stone the builders rejected has become the capstone; the Lord has done this, and it is marvelous in our eyes. This is the day the Lord has made; let us rejoice and be glad in it.

CHOIR: "His love endures forever."

TESTIMONY 5: O Lord, save us; O Lord grant us success. Blessed is he who comes in the name of the Lord. From the house of the Lord we bless you. The Lord is God, and he has made his light shine upon us. With boughs in hand, join in the festal procession up to the horns of the altar.

LEADER: You are my God, and I will give you thanks;

CHOIR: You are my God, and I will exalt you.

LEADER: Give thanks to the Lord, for he is good;

CHOIR: His love endures forever.

Script and/or Scripture arrangement from *The Psalms in Worship,* by Miller and Wyatt, © 1995. All rights reserved by Lillenas Publishing Company. Scripture quotes and paraphrases are from the *Holy Bible, New International Version®* (NIV®). Copyright © 1973, 1978, 1984 by International Bible Society. Used by permission of Zondervan Publishing House. All rights reserved.

Psalm 119

(vv. 9-16)

MALE LEADER: How can a young man keep his way pure?

CHOIR MEN: By living according to your word.

TEEN BOY: I seek you with all my heart; do not let me stray from your commands.

CHOIR MEN: I have hidden your word in my heart that I might not sin against you.

MALE LEADER: Praise be to you, O Lord;

TEEN BOY: Teach me your decrees.

CHOIR MEN: With my lips I recount all the laws that come from your mouth.

TEEN BOY: I rejoice in following your statutes as one rejoices in great riches. I meditate on your precepts and consider your ways.

CHOIR MEN: I delight in your decrees;

ALL: I will not neglect your word.

Script and/or Scripture arrangement from *The Psalms in Worship*, by Miller and Wyatt, © 1995. All rights reserved by Lillenas Publishing Company. Scripture quotes and paraphrases are from the *Holy Bible, New International Version*® (NIV®). Copyright © 1973, 1978, 1984 by International Bible Society. Used by permission of Zondervan Publishing House. All rights reserved.

Psalm 119

(vv. 33-40)

LEADER: Teach me, O Lord, to follow your decrees;

PEOPLE: Then I will keep them to the end.

LEADER: Give me understanding,

PEOPLE: And I will keep your law and obey it with all my heart.

LEADER: Direct me in the path of your commands,

PEOPLE: For there I find delight.

LEADER: Turn my heart toward your statutes

PEOPLE: And not toward selfish gain.

LEADER: Turn my eyes away from worthless things;

PEOPLE: Preserve my life according to your word.

LEADER: Fulfill your promise to your servant,

PEOPLE: So that you may be feared.

LEADER: Take away the disgrace I dread,

PEOPLE: For your laws are good.

LEADER: How I long for your precepts!

PEOPLE: Preserve my life in your righteousness.

Script and/or Scripture arrangement from *The Psalms in Worship*, by Miller and Wyatt, © 1995. All rights reserved by Lillenas Publishing Company. Scripture quotes and paraphrases are from the *Holy Bible, New International Version*® (NIV®). Copyright © 1973, 1978, 1984 by International Bible Society. Used by permission of Zondervan Publishing House. All rights reserved.

Psalm 119

(vv. 41-48)

FEMALE LEADER: Love for God is the theme of Psalm 119, verses 41 through 48.

FEMALE SOLO: May your unfailing love come to me, O Lord, your salvation according to your promise;

CHOIR WOMEN: Then I will answer the one who taunts me,

FEMALE SOLO: For I trust in your word.

FEMALE LEADER: Do not snatch the word of truth from my mouth, for I have put my hope in your laws.

CHOIR WOMEN: I will always obey your law, for ever and ever.

FEMALE SOLO: I will walk about in freedom, for I have sought out your precepts. I will speak of your statutes before kings and will not be put to shame, for I delight in your commands because I love them. I lift up my hands to your commands,

CHOIR WOMEN: Which I love,

FEMALE SOLO: And I meditate on your decrees.

FEMALE LEADER: May your unfailing love come to me.

ALL: Your salvation according to your promise.

Script and/or Scripture arrangement from *The Psalms in Worship,* by Miller and Wyatt, © 1995. All rights reserved by Lillenas Publishing Company. Scripture quotes and paraphrases are from the *Holy Bible, New International Version*® (NIV®). Copyright © 1973, 1978, 1984 by International Bible Society. Used by permission of Zondervan Publishing House. All rights reserved.

Psalm 119

(vv. 105-112)

LEADER: I have taken an oath and confirmed it, that I will follow your righteous laws.

RIGHT: Your word is a lamp to my feet.

LEFT: Your word is a light for my path.

LEADER: I have suffered much; preserve my life, O Lord, according to your word.

RIGHT: Your word is a lamp to my feet.

LEFT: Your word is a light for my path.

LEADER: Accept, O Lord, the willing praise of my mouth, and teach me your laws.

RIGHT: Your word is a lamp to my feet.

LEFT: Your word is a light for my path.

LEADER: Though I constantly take my life in my hands, I will not forget your law.

RIGHT: Your word is a lamp to my feet.

LEFT: Your word is a light for my path.

LEADER: The wicked have set a snare for me, but I have not strayed from your precepts.

RIGHT: Your word is a lamp to my feet.

LEFT: Your word is a light for my path.

LEADER: Your statutes are my heritage forever; they are the joy of my heart.

RIGHT: Your word is a lamp to my feet.

LEFT: Your word is a light for my path.

LEADER: My heart is set on keeping your decrees to the very end.

ALL: Your word is a lamp to my feet and a light for my path.

Script and/or Scripture arrangement from *The Psalms in Worship*, by Miller and Wyatt, © 1995. All rights reserved by Lillenas Publishing Company. Scripture quotes and paraphrases are from the *Holy Bible, New International Version*® (NIV®). Copyright © 1973, 1978, 1984 by International Bible Society. Used by permission of Zondervan Publishing House. All rights reserved.

Psalm 119

(vv. 145-152)

LEADER: Long ago I learned from your statutes that you established them to last forever.

RIGHT: I call with all my heart;

LEFT: Answer me, O Lord, and I will obey your decrees.

RIGHT: I call out to you;

LEFT: Save me and I will keep your statutes.

RIGHT: I rise before dawn and cry for help;

LEFT: I have put my hope in your word.

RIGHT: My eyes stay open through the watches of the night,

LEFT: That I may meditate on your promises.

RIGHT: Hear my voice in accordance with your love;

LEFT: Preserve my life, O Lord, according to your laws.

LEADER: Those who devise wicked schemes are near, but they are far from your law.

PEOPLE: Yet you are near, O Lord.

LEADER: Long ago I learned from your statutes that you established them to last forever.

PEOPLE: O Lord, all your commands are true.

Script and/or Scripture arrangement from *The Psalms in Worship*, by Miller and Wyatt, © 1995. All rights reserved by Lillenas Publishing Company. Scripture quotes and paraphrases are from the *Holy Bible, New International Version*® (NIV®). Copyright © 1973, 1978, 1984 by International Bible Society. Used by permission of Zondervan Publishing House. All rights reserved.

Psalm 121

LEADER: I lift up my eyes to the hills—

PEOPLE: Where does my help come from?

LEADER: My help comes from the Lord.

CHOIR: The Lord, the Maker of heaven and earth.

MEN: He will not let your foot slip—

WOMEN: He watches over you.

PEOPLE: He will not slumber;

LEADER: He who watches over Israel will neither slumber nor sleep.

CHOIR: The Lord watches over you—

LEADER: The Lord is your shade on your right hand;

MEN: The sun will not harm you by day,

WOMEN: Nor the moon by night.

LEADER: The Lord will keep you from all harm—

CHOIR: He will watch over your life;

MEN: The Lord will watch over your coming.

WOMEN: The Lord will watch over your going

PEOPLE: Both now and forever.

Script and/or Scripture arrangement from *The Psalms in Worship,* by Miller and Wyatt, © 1995. All rights reserved by Lillenas Publishing Company. Scripture quotes and paraphrases are from the *Holy Bible, New International Version*® (NIV®). Copyright © 1973, 1978, 1984 by International Bible Society. Used by permission of Zondervan Publishing House. All rights reserved.

Psalm 121

Solo 1: I lift up my eyes to the hills—

Solo 2: Where does my help come from?

All: My help comes from the Lord, the Maker of heaven and earth.

Solo 1: He will not let your foot slip—

Solo 2: He who watches over you will not slumber;

All: Indeed, he who watches over Israel will neither slumber nor sleep.

Solo 1: The Lord watches over you—

Solo 2: The Lord is your shade at your right hand;

All: The sun will not harm you by day, nor the moon by night.

Solo 1: The Lord will keep you from all harm—

Solo 2: He will watch over your life;

All: The Lord will watch over your coming and going both now and forevermore.

Script and/or Scripture arrangement from *The Psalms in Worship*, by Miller and Wyatt, © 1995. All rights reserved by Lillenas Publishing Company. Scripture quotes and paraphrases are from the *Holy Bible, New International Version*® (NIV®). Copyright © 1973, 1978, 1984 by International Bible Society. Used by permission of Zondervan Publishing House. All rights reserved.

Psalm 122

LEADER: I rejoiced with those who said to me, "Let us go to the house of the Lord."

PEOPLE: Our feet are standing in your gates, O Jerusalem.

LEADER: Jerusalem is built like a city that is closely compacted together.

PEOPLE: That is where the tribes go up,

WOMEN: The tribes of the Lord,

PEOPLE: To praise the name of the Lord

MEN: According to the statute given to Israel.

LEADER: There the thrones for judgment stand,

PEOPLE: The thrones of the house of David.

LEADER: Pray for the peace of Jerusalem:

PEOPLE: "May those who love you be secure.

WOMEN: "May there be peace within your walls

MEN: "And security within your citadels."

LEADER: For the sake of my brothers and friends, I will say,

PEOPLE: "Peace be within you."

LEADER: For the sake of the house of the Lord our God,

PEOPLE: I will seek your prosperity.

Script and/or Scripture arrangement from *The Psalms in Worship*, by Miller and Wyatt, © 1995. All rights reserved by Lillenas Publishing Company. Scripture quotes and paraphrases are from the *Holy Bible, New International Version*® (NIV®). Copyright © 1973, 1978, 1984 by International Bible Society. Used by permission of Zondervan Publishing House. All rights reserved.

Psalm 124

Solo 1: If the Lord had not been on our side—let Israel say—

Solo 2: If the Lord had not been on our side when men attacked us,

All: When their anger flared against us, they would have swallowed us alive;

Solo 1: The flood would have engulfed us, the torrent would have swept over us,

Solo 2: The raging waters would have swept us away.

All: Praise be to the Lord, who has not let us be torn by their teeth.

Solo 1: We have escaped like a bird out of the fowler's snare;

Solo 2: The snare has been broken, and we have escaped.

All: Our help is in the name of the Lord, the Maker of heaven and earth.

Script and/or Scripture arrangement from *The Psalms in Worship,* by Miller and Wyatt, © 1995. All rights reserved by Lillenas Publishing Company. Scripture quotes and paraphrases are from the *Holy Bible, New International Version*® (NIV®). Copyright © 1973, 1978, 1984 by International Bible Society. Used by permission of Zondervan Publishing House. All rights reserved.

Psalm 127

LEADER: Unless the Lord builds the house,

PEOPLE: Its builders labor in vain.

LEADER: Unless the Lord watches over the city,

PEOPLE: The watchmen stand guard in vain.

MEN: In vain you rise early

WOMEN: And stay up late,

MEN: Toiling for food to eat—

WOMEN: For he grants sleep to those he loves.

LEADER: Sons are a heritage from the Lord,

PEOPLE: Children a reward from him.

LEADER: Like arrows in the hands of a warrior

PEOPLE: Are sons born in one's youth.

LEADER: Blessed is the man

PEOPLE: Whose quiver is full of them.

LEADER: They will not be put to shame

PEOPLE: When they contend with their enemies in the gate.

Script and/or Scripture arrangement from *The Psalms in Worship*, by Miller and Wyatt, © 1995. All rights reserved by Lillenas Publishing Company. Scripture quotes and paraphrases are from the *Holy Bible, New International Version* (NIV®). Copyright © 1973, 1978, 1984 by International Bible Society. Used by permission of Zondervan Publishing House. All rights reserved.

Psalm 128

LEADER: Blessed are all who fear the Lord,

PEOPLE: Who walk in his ways.

LEADER: You will eat the fruit of your labor;

PEOPLE: Blessings and prosperity will be yours.

LEADER: Your wife will be like a fruitful vine within your house;

PEOPLE: Your sons will be like olive shoots around your table.

LEADER: Thus is the man blessed who fears the Lord.

PEOPLE: May the Lord bless you from Zion all the days of your life;

LEADER: May you see the prosperity of Jerusalem,

PEOPLE: And may you live to see your children's children.

ALL: Peace be upon Israel.

Script and/or Scripture arrangement from *The Psalms in Worship*, by Miller and Wyatt, © 1995. All rights reserved by Lillenas Publishing Company. Scripture quotes and paraphrases are from the *Holy Bible, New International Version*® (NIV®). Copyright © 1973, 1978, 1984 by International Bible Society. Used by permission of Zondervan Publishing House. All rights reserved.

Psalm 130

LEADER: Psalm 130 assures God's forgiveness.

SOLO 1: Out of the depths I cry to you, O Lord.

SOLO 2: Let your ears be attentive to my cry for mercy.

SOLO 1: If you, O Lord, kept a record of sins,

SOLO 2: O Lord, who could stand?

SOLO 1: But with you there is forgiveness;

SOLO 2: Therefore you are feared.

SOLO 1: I wait for the Lord, my soul waits, and in his word I put my hope.

SOLO 2: My soul waits for the Lord more than watchmen wait for the morning,

SOLO 1: More than watchmen wait for the morning.

LEADER: O Israel, put your hope in the Lord,

SOLO 2: For with the Lord is unfailing love

SOLO 1: And with him is full redemption.

LEADER: He himself will redeem Israel.

ALL: He himself will redeem Israel from all their sins.

Script and/or Scripture arrangement from *The Psalms in Worship,* by Miller and Wyatt, © 1995. All rights reserved by Lillenas Publishing Company. Scripture quotes and paraphrases are from the *Holy Bible, New International Version*® (NIV®). Copyright © 1973, 1978, 1984 by International Bible Society. Used by permission of Zondervan Publishing House. All rights reserved.

Psalm 133

LEADER: How good and pleasant it is when brothers live together in unity!

WOMEN: It is like precious oil poured on the head,

MEN: Running down on the beard,

WOMEN: Running down on Aaron's beard,

MEN: Down upon the collar of his robes.

LEADER: It is as if the dew of Hermon were falling on Mount Zion.

ALL: For there the Lord bestows his blessing, even life forevermore.

Script and/or Scripture arrangement from *The Psalms in Worship,* by Miller and Wyatt, © 1995. All rights reserved by Lillenas Publishing Company. Scripture quotes and paraphrases are from the *Holy Bible, New International Version*® (NIV®). Copyright © 1973, 1978, 1984 by International Bible Society. Used by permission of Zondervan Publishing House. All rights reserved.

Psalm 134

LEADER: Praise the Lord, all you servants of the Lord who minister by night in the house of the Lord.

PEOPLE: Praise the Lord!

LEADER: Lift up your hands in the sanctuary and praise the Lord.

PEOPLE: Praise the Lord!

LEADER: May the Lord, the Maker of heaven and earth, bless you from Zion.

PEOPLE: Praise the Lord!

Script and/or Scripture arrangement from *The Psalms in Worship,* by Miller and Wyatt, © 1995. All rights reserved by Lillenas Publishing Company. Scripture quotes and paraphrases are from the *Holy Bible, New International Version*® (NIV®). Copyright © 1973, 1978, 1984 by International Bible Society. Used by permission of Zondervan Publishing House. All rights reserved.

Psalm 136

(vv. 1-18, 21-26)

LEADER: Give thanks to the Lord, for he is good.

PEOPLE: His love endures forever.

LEADER: Give thanks to the God of gods.

PEOPLE: His love endures forever.

LEADER: Give thanks to the Lord of lords:

PEOPLE: His love endures forever.

WOMEN: To him who alone does great wonders,

PEOPLE: His love endures forever.

WOMEN: Who by his understanding made the heavens,

PEOPLE: His love endures forever.

WOMEN: Who spread out the earth upon the waters,

PEOPLE: His love endures forever.

WOMEN: Who made the great lights—

PEOPLE: His love endures forever.

WOMEN: The sun to govern the day,

PEOPLE: His love endures forever.

WOMEN: The moon and stars to govern the night;

PEOPLE: His love endures forever.

LEADER: To him who struck down the firstborn of Egypt

PEOPLE: His love endures forever.

LEADER: And brought Israel out from among them

PEOPLE: His love endures forever.

LEADER: With a mighty hand and outstretched arm;

PEOPLE: His love endures forever.

LEADER: To him who divided the Red Sea asunder

PEOPLE: His love endures forever.

LEADER: And brought Israel through the midst of it,

PEOPLE: His love endures forever.

MEN: To him who led his people through the desert,

PEOPLE: His love endures forever.

MEN: Who struck down great kings,

PEOPLE: His love endures forever.

MEN: And killed mighty kings—

PEOPLE: His love endures forever.

MEN: And gave their land as an inheritance,

PEOPLE: His love endures forever.

MEN: An inheritance to his servant Israel;

PEOPLE: His love endures forever.

LEADER: To the One who remembered us in our low estate

PEOPLE: His love endures forever.

LEADER: And freed us from our enemies,

PEOPLE: His love endures forever.

LEADER: And who gives food to every creature.

PEOPLE: His love endures forever.

LEADER: Give thanks to the God of heaven.

PEOPLE: His love endures forever.

Script and/or Scripture arrangement from *The Psalms in Worship,* by Miller and Wyatt, © 1995. All rights reserved by Lillenas Publishing Company. Scripture quotes and paraphrases are from the *Holy Bible, New International Version*® (NIV®). Copyright © 1973, 1978, 1984 by International Bible Society. Used by permission of Zondervan Publishing House. All rights reserved.

Psalm 137

(vv. 1-6)

LEADER: Psalm 137 expresses the sorrow of a person in exile weeping over the bitterness of captivity.

SOLO 1: By the rivers of Babylon we sat and wept when we remembered Zion.

SOLO 2: There on the poplars we hung our harps,

SOLO 1: For there our captors asked us for songs,

SOLO 2: Our tormentors demanded songs of joy; they said, "Sing us one of the songs of Zion!"

SOLO 1: "Sing us one of the songs of Zion!" How can we sing the songs of the Lord while in a foreign land?

SOLO 2: If I forget you, O Jerusalem,

SOLO 1: May my right hand forget its skill.

SOLO 2: If I forget you, O Jerusalem,

SOLO 1: May my tongue cling to the roof of my mouth if I do not remember you,

SOLO 2: If I do not consider Jerusalem my highest joy.

Script and/or Scripture arrangement from *The Psalms in Worship,* by Miller and Wyatt, © 1995. All rights reserved by Lillenas Publishing Company. Scripture quotes and paraphrases are from the *Holy Bible, New International Version*® (NIV®). Copyright © 1973, 1978, 1984 by International Bible Society. Used by permission of Zondervan Publishing House. All rights reserved.

Captives in Babylon
Psalm 137

A Readers Theatre Interpretation

WOMAN 1: There are rivers that run through life.

WOMAN 2: Rivers that run as swiftly as the good times of life.

MAN 1 *(as a boy):* Boy, Dad, howdya know I wanted a bike like this?

MAN 2: Well, it wasn't hard to figure out. You've been talking about it all year.

WOMAN 2: And those ads you've been taping to the bathroom mirror? They kind of gave us a clue.

MAN 2: And you talked to the Lord about it so much at family prayers, well . . .

MAN 1 *(as a boy):* Boy, you guys are pretty sharp!

WOMAN 2: Some of the rivers of life overflow the channels of our hopes and dreams.

WOMAN 1: Oh, Mom, he's the nicest person. He's good and kind and honest and thoughtful and . . .

WOMAN 2: He's a Boy Scout?

WOMAN 1 *(ignoring her):* And he's asked me to marry him.

WOMAN 2: Oh, honey!

WOMAN 1: What's the matter, Mom; aren't you happy for me?

WOMAN 2: Of course I am, dear. Just give me a bit to catch my breath and remember that my girl is all grown up.

WOMAN 1: Well, sometimes I am. Oh, Mom, he's so wonderful!

MAN 1: The currents of life move swiftly and run deeply.

MAN 2: They find us in all the corners of our life. When we least expect, we can be buoyed to a high plateau of joy . . .

MAN 1: Or, we can be swept into the depths of despair and nearly drown in our sorrow.

[Begin optional instrumental underscoring.]

WOMAN 2: "By the rivers of Babylon . . ."

MAN 2: "By the rivers of Babylon we sat and wept."

MAN 1: "We sat and wept when we remembered Zion."

WOMAN 1: Oh, the rivers of Babylon.

MAN 1: Babylon—that pagan place of Israel's exile,

WOMAN 2: When they were taken from their beloved Zion,

MAN 2: And made to live in captivity.

WOMAN 1: "By the rivers of Babylon we sat and wept when we remembered Zion."

MAN 1: There is no music in the exiled heart.

MAN 2: There is no melody beneath the trees that trail their branches in the rivers of Babylon.

WOMAN 2: "There on the poplars we hung our harps, for there our captors asked us for songs."

WOMAN 1: "Our tormentors demanded songs of joy;"

MAN 1 and 2: "'Sing us one of the songs of Zion!'"

WOMAN 1: "How can we sing the songs of the Lord while in a foreign land?"

[Optional instrumental underscoring begins to play "Sweet Hour of Prayer."]

WOMAN 1: "The songs of the Lord," those are songs that remind us of the times of our lives.

[SOLOIST, *accompanied by underscoring, softly and with great simplicity begins to sing "Sweet Hour of Prayer."*]

WOMAN 2 *(over music):* "How can we sing the songs of the Lord when we are exiled by our sorrow and unhappiness?

MAN 2: How can we sing the songs of the Lord when He seems to be as far away as Zion?

MAN 1: Let my right hand forget how to play the harp,

WOMAN 1: Let my tongue be unable to sing any more,

WOMAN 2: If I forget Zion.

[Song ends and underscoring continues under the following.]

Man 1: "If I forget Zion . . ."

Woman 2: If I forget the goodness of God . . .

Man 2: If I forget the depth of His love . . .

Woman 1: And the currents of His promises

Man 1: By your river of Babylon, "I will not forget you."

All: Amen.

Script and/or Scripture arrangement from *The Psalms in Worship*, by Miller and Wyatt, © 1995. All rights reserved by Lillenas Publishing Company. Scripture quotes and paraphrases are from the *Holy Bible, New International Version*® (NIV®). Copyright © 1973, 1978, 1984 by International Bible Society. Used by permission of Zondervan Publishing House. All rights reserved.

Psalm 139

(vv. 1-3, 23-24)

LEADER: Search me, O God, and know my heart.

PEOPLE: O Lord, you have searched me and you know me.

LEADER: Test me and know my anxious thoughts.

PEOPLE: You know when I sit and when I rise; you perceive my thoughts from afar.

LEADER: See if there is any offensive way in me.

PEOPLE: You discern my going out and my lying down; you are familiar with all my ways.

ALL: O God, lead me in the way everlasting.

Script and/or Scripture arrangement from *The Psalms in Worship*, by Miller and Wyatt, © 1995. All rights reserved by Lillenas Publishing Company. Scripture quotes and paraphrases are from the *Holy Bible, New International Version*® (NIV®). Copyright © 1973, 1978, 1984 by International Bible Society. Used by permission of Zondervan Publishing House. All rights reserved.

Psalm 139

(vv. 7-10)

LEADER: O Lord, where can I go from your Spirit? Where can I flee from your presence?

PEOPLE: If I go up to the heavens, you are there;

LEADER: If I make my bed in the depths, you are there.

WOMEN: If I rise on the wings of the dawn,

MEN: If I settle on the far side of the sea,

LEADER: Even there your hand will guide me,

PEOPLE: Your hand will hold me fast.

Script and/or Scripture arrangement from *The Psalms in Worship*, by Miller and Wyatt, © 1995. All rights reserved by Lillenas Publishing Company. Scripture quotes and paraphrases are from the *Holy Bible, New International Version*® (NIV®). Copyright © 1973, 1978, 1984 by International Bible Society. Used by permission of Zondervan Publishing House. All rights reserved.

Psalm 144

LEADER: Praise be to the Lord my Rock, who trains my hands for war, my fingers for battle.

RIGHT: He is my loving God and my fortress, my stronghold and my deliverer,

LEFT: My shield, in whom I take refuge, who subdues peoples under me.

LEADER: O Lord, what is man that you care for him, the son of man that you think of him?

RIGHT: Man is like a breath;

LEFT: His days are like a fleeting shadow.

RIGHT: Part your heavens, O Lord, and come down;

LEFT: Touch the mountains, so that they smoke.

RIGHT: Send forth lightning and scatter the enemies;

LEFT: Shoot your arrows and rout them.

RIGHT: Reach down your hand from on high.

LEFT: Deliver me and rescue me from the mighty waters.

LEADER: Deliver me and rescue me from the hands of foreigners whose mouths are full of lies, whose right hands are deceitful.

RIGHT: I will sing a new song to you, O God;

LEFT: On the ten-stringed lyre I will make music to you,

RIGHT: To the One who gives victory to kings,

LEFT: Who delivers his servant David from the deadly sword.

LEADER: Deliver me and rescue me from the hands of foreigners whose mouths are full of lies, whose right hands are deceitful.

RIGHT: Then our sons in their youth will be like well-nurtured plants.

LEFT: Then our daughters will be like pillars carved to adorn a palace.

RIGHT: Our barns will be filled with every kind of provision.

LEFT: Our sheep will increase by thousands, by tens of thousands in our fields;

RIGHT: Our oxen will draw heavy loads.

LEFT: There will be no breaching of walls.

RIGHT: There will be no going into captivity.

LEFT: There will be no cry of distress in our streets.

RIGHT: Blessed are the people of whom this is true;

LEFT: Blessed are the people whose God is the Lord.

Script and/or Scripture arrangement from *The Psalms in Worship*, by Miller and Wyatt, © 1995. All rights reserved by Lillenas Publishing Company. Scripture quotes and paraphrases are from the *Holy Bible, New International Version®* (NIV®). Copyright © 1973, 1978, 1984 by International Bible Society. Used by permission of Zondervan Publishing House. All rights reserved.

Psalm 149 and 67

(149:1-2, 4, 6; 67:4-5)

LEADER: May the peoples praise you, O God;

PEOPLE: May all the peoples praise you.

LEADER: Sing to the Lord a new song, his praise in the assembly of the saints.

MEN: Let Israel rejoice in their Maker;

WOMEN: Let the people of Zion be glad in their King.

PEOPLE: For the Lord takes delight in his people;

LEADER: He crowns the humble with salvation.

PEOPLE: May the praise of God be in their mouths.

LEADER: May the nations be glad and sing for joy,

MEN: For you rule the peoples justly

WOMEN: And guide the nations of the earth.

LEADER: May the peoples praise you,

PEOPLE: O God; may all the peoples praise you.

Script and/or Scripture arrangement from *The Psalms in Worship*, by Miller and Wyatt, © 1995. All rights reserved by Lillenas Publishing Company. Scripture quotes and paraphrases are from the *Holy Bible, New International Version®* (NIV®). Copyright © 1973, 1978, 1984 by International Bible Society. Used by permission of Zondervan Publishing House. All rights reserved.

Psalm 150

[Organ or brass fanfare]

LEADER: Praise the Lord.

CHOIR: Praise the Lord.

ALL: Praise the Lord.

LEADER: Praise God in his sanctuary;

PEOPLE: Praise him in his mighty heavens

CHOIR: Praise him for his acts of power;

ALL: Praise him for his surpassing greatness.

[Simple brass fanfare]

LEADER: Praise him with the sounding of the trumpet,

[Glissando or arpeggio-type chord on organ.]

PEOPLE: Praise him with the harp and lyre,

[Organ continues under following; choir clap open hand across the palm of other hand in rhythm.]

LEADER: Praise him with tambourine and dancing,

[Continue organ music with flute or string stops.]

PEOPLE: Praise him with the strings and flute,

[Choir claps three unison claps, circling their hands between each clap.]

ALL: Praise him with the clash of cymbals.

LEADER: Let everything that has breath praise the Lord.

[Organ plays three chords; one under each word in the following; choir may clap under the three words.]

ALL: Praise the Lord.

Script and/or Scripture arrangement from *The Psalms in Worship*, by Miller and Wyatt, © 1995. All rights reserved by Lillenas Publishing Company. Scripture quotes and paraphrases are from the *Holy Bible, New International Version*® (NIV®). Copyright © 1973, 1978, 1984 by International Bible Society. Used by permission of Zondervan Publishing House. All rights reserved.

Service Responses

Praise

(134:1-2; 148:13-14)

LEADER: Praise the Lord, all you servants of the Lord.

PEOPLE: Lift up your hands in the sanctuary.

LEADER: Lift up your hands and praise the Lord.

PEOPLE: His name alone is exalted;

MEN: His splendor is above the earth.

WOMEN: His splendor is above the heavens.

PEOPLE: Praise the Lord.

Script and/or Scripture arrangement from *The Psalms in Worship*, by Miller and Wyatt, © 1995. All rights reserved by Lillenas Publishing Company. Scripture quotes and paraphrases are from the *Holy Bible, New International Version*® (NIV®). Copyright © 1973, 1978, 1984 by International Bible Society. Used by permission of Zondervan Publishing House. All rights reserved.

Thanksgiving

(30:2, 11-12)

LEADER: O Lord my God, I called to you for help and you healed me.

PEOPLE: You turned my wailing into dancing;

LEADER: You removed my sackcloth and clothed me with joy, that my heart may sing to you and not be silent.

PEOPLE: O Lord my God, I will give you thanks forever.

Script and/or Scripture arrangement from *The Psalms in Worship*, by Miller and Wyatt, © 1995. All rights reserved by Lillenas Publishing Company. Scripture quotes and paraphrases are from the *Holy Bible, New International Version*® (NIV®). Copyright © 1973, 1978, 1984 by International Bible Society. Used by permission of Zondervan Publishing House. All rights reserved.

Call to Worship
(29:2; 100:2)

LEADER: Worship the Lord in the splendor of his holiness.

PEOPLE: Worship the Lord with gladness; come before him with joyful songs.

Script and/or Scripture arrangement from *The Psalms in Worship,* by Miller and Wyatt, © 1995. All rights reserved by Lillenas Publishing Company. Scripture quotes and paraphrases are from the *Holy Bible, New International Version*® (NIV®). Copyright © 1973, 1978, 1984 by International Bible Society. Used by permission of Zondervan Publishing House. All rights reserved.

Call to Worship
(19:14)

LEADER: May the words of my mouth

PEOPLE: And the meditation of my heart

LEADER: Be pleasing in your sight,

PEOPLE: O Lord, my Rock and my Redeemer.

Script and/or Scripture arrangement from *The Psalms in Worship,* by Miller and Wyatt, © 1995. All rights reserved by Lillenas Publishing Company. Scripture quotes and paraphrases are from the *Holy Bible, New International Version*® (NIV®). Copyright © 1973, 1978, 1984 by International Bible Society. Used by permission of Zondervan Publishing House. All rights reserved.

Call to Worship
(118:24)

LEADER: This is the day the Lord has made;

PEOPLE: Let us rejoice and be glad in it.

Script and/or Scripture arrangement from *The Psalms in Worship,* by Miller and Wyatt, © 1995. All rights reserved by Lillenas Publishing Company. Scripture quotes and paraphrases are from the *Holy Bible, New International Version*® (NIV®). Copyright © 1973, 1978, 1984 by International Bible Society. Used by permission of Zondervan Publishing House. All rights reserved.

Call to Worship
(34:3)

LEADER: Glorify the Lord with me;

PEOPLE: Let us exalt his name together.

Script and/or Scripture arrangement from *The Psalms in Worship*, by Miller and Wyatt, © 1995. All rights reserved by Lillenas Publishing Company. Scripture quotes and paraphrases are from the *Holy Bible, New International Version*® (NIV®). Copyright © 1973, 1978, 1984 by International Bible Society. Used by permission of Zondervan Publishing House. All rights reserved.

A Response
(96:4)

LEADER: Great is the Lord

PEOPLE: And most worthy of praise.

Script and/or Scripture arrangement from *The Psalms in Worship*, by Miller and Wyatt, © 1995. All rights reserved by Lillenas Publishing Company. Scripture quotes and paraphrases are from the *Holy Bible, New International Version*® (NIV®). Copyright © 1973, 1978, 1984 by International Bible Society. Used by permission of Zondervan Publishing House. All rights reserved.

A Response
(84:11)

LEADER: The Lord God is a sun and shield;

PEOPLE: The Lord bestows favor and honor;

LEADER: No good thing does he withhold

PEOPLE: From those whose walk is blameless.

Script and/or Scripture arrangement from *The Psalms in Worship*, by Miller and Wyatt, © 1995. All rights reserved by Lillenas Publishing Company. Scripture quotes and paraphrases are from the *Holy Bible, New International Version*® (NIV®). Copyright © 1973, 1978, 1984 by International Bible Society. Used by permission of Zondervan Publishing House. All rights reserved.

Topical Index

Confidence .... Psalms 3, 27, 34, 124

Deliverence .... Psalms 6, 9, 18, 34, 46, 56, 82, 88, 107, 124, 137, 144

Desire for God .... Psalms 63, 86, 88, 130, 137

God

    Answers Prayer .... Psalm 66

    Care, His .... Psalms 8, 23, 29, 56, 61, 71, 84, 95, 103, 112, 113, 115, 121, 124, 139, 149

    Eternal Nature .... Psalms 90, 93, 117, 118

    Faithfulness .... Psalms 36, 53, 57, 89, 100, 117, 144

    Forgiveness .... Psalms 51, 53, 103, 130

    Good Shepherd .... Psalms 23, 95, 100

    Greatness .... Psalms 19, 47, 86, 97, 113, 115

    Guidance .... Psalms 23, 119

    Holiness .... Psalms 24, 73, 93

    Hope .... Psalm 71

    In Nature .... Psalms 29, 65, 93, 97

    Judgment .... Psalms 82, 110

    Justice .... Psalms 36, 82, 107

    Kingship .... Psalms 47, 57

    Love .... Psalms 36, 51, 62, 86, 89, 100, 103, 107, 117, 118, 139

    Mercy .... Psalms 39, 51, 53, 57, 113

    Ownership .... Psalms 24, 47

    Preeminence .... Psalms 14, 37, 66, 95, 97, 111, 115

    Protection .... Psalms 4, 27, 46, 61, 71, 95, 107, 113, 121

    Provision .... Psalms 65, 112, 119, 127, 128

    Will .... Psalm 40

Word	Psalm 119
Joys and Benefits	Psalms 16, 27, 37, 67, 84, 86, 95, 113, 118, 128, 133, 149
Marriage	Psalm 128
Patience	Psalm 40
Peace	Psalm 122
Praise	Psalms 67, 71, 84, 100, 103, 117, 134, 136
Relief from Despair	Psalms 13, 22, 42
Righteous, The	Psalms 1, 15, 37, 73, 107, 112, 119, 128
Seeking God	Psalms 39, 42, 51, 53, 62, 63, 139
Sorrow for Sin	Psalms 38, 51

Special Days

(See Lectionary)

Advent	Psalms 24, 50, 72, 80, 85, 110, 118, 122, 126, 132
Christmas	Psalms 96, 97, 98
Holy Week	Psalms 22, 118
Easter	Psalms 22, 36, 40, 69, 71, 78, 114, 118, 130, 136
Pentecost	Psalms 33, 104, 130
Stewardship	Psalms 24, 112
Thanksgiving	Psalms 65, 100, 107, 118, 136, 150
Trust	Psalms 37, 56, 84